FROM A
ROCK
TO A
HARD
PLACE

FROM A ROCK TO A HARD PLACE

Memories of the 1984/85 MINERS' STRIKE

BEVERLEY TROUNCE

WITH A CONTRIBUTION BY EX-STRIKING MINER CHARLIE CIBOR

The History Press

For the striking miners and their families – they know who they are

This living coal just sits and waits
for man alone to seal its fate.
We scoop it up to light the fire
Its heart, it glows, for our desire.
And when it's dead we clear it out,
Like miners' jobs, its heart ripped out.
This living coal that filled our needs,
Like miners' lives, it's done its deed.

(From a poem by Peter Curry, ex-striking miner, Markham Main Colliery)

Cover illustrations: front, courtesy of Bruce Wilson;
back, courtesy of Peter Arkell.

First published 2015

The History Press
The Mill, Brimscombe Port
Stroud, Gloucestershire, GL5 2QG
www.thehistorypress.co.uk

British Library Cataloguing in Publication Data.
A catalogue record for this book is available from the British Library.

ISBN 978 0 7509 6201 8

Typesetting and origination by The History Press
Printed in Great Britain

CONTENTS

ACKNOWLEDGEMENTS

With grateful thanks to Peter Arkell, Bruce Wilson, Ian Wroe, John Trounce, Don Utley, Graham Reeves, David Bell, Mick Stowe; Chris Skidmore and Richard Riggs at the NUM; David Ayrton, Ian Sternberg, Leslie and Jean Phillips; Sean McKernan, Head of Library and Learning Support Centre, Northern College; Rob and Ellie Trounce for their patient computer tuition; Paul Mackney; and to all those who have so generously allowed me into their lives to share their memories. All images are from the author's collection unless otherwise credited.

INTRODUCTION

My father had been a miner before I was born and so I grew up hearing the tales he had to tell of his life underground. During the 1980s I was working as a librarian in a Nottinghamshire mining area where the colliery had always been the lifeblood of the community. This was, however, the beginning of the end of an era. Within the next few years this community, along with many others, would face huge upheaval and, in many cases, the end of a generations-old way of life. The closing down of the collieries and the strike of 1984/5 would become, for them, the defining events of that decade.

The miners and their families were forced to shape new identities for themselves and make their way in a world no longer dominated by their colliery. They were witnessing not only their pits closing down but also the collapse of their society. Communities that had been bound by their coal mine now had to separate and individuals had to follow their own path, forging ahead in a world where rules of the old way of life no longer applied. Some never recovered. Marriages ended, families were split and friendships destroyed. The memories, though, remain and, thirty years on, there are still stories to tell.

FOREWORD

by Ken Capstick

The former Chinese premier, Chou En Lai, was once asked, in the late 1970s, what he thought was the significance of the French Revolution of 1789 almost 200 years earlier. His answer was highly significant. He said, 'It is too soon to say.'

Thirty years on from the Great Miners' Strike of 1984/85 the same thing can be said. It seems with every passing year that the great struggle of the miners and their families takes on a higher significance, one that validates not only the reasons for the strike, but also the leadership of it.

The Great Miners' Strike will go down in history as a working-class struggle to stand alongside the great endeavours of the past, from Watt Tyler's Peasants' Revolt to the pains of the Levellers, the Diggers, the Chartists and the suffragettes. The coal mines may be gone, but in their place is something that will live on longer than the mines ever would. The struggle will live on in the collective memories of working-class people, as will the dignity of those who so heroically took part.

As Arthur Scargill so often reminds us all, 'The victory is in the struggle itself.'

Ken Capstick, former Vice-President NUM (Yorkshire Area)

FOREWORD

by Peter Arkell

The year-long miners' strike of 1984/5 for jobs was a rare kind of confrontation. The feeling that a terrible injustice was forced on to the 180,000 miners of the time keeps on growing. There are now hardly any deep mines left in Britain and the former thriving communities have largely collapsed. Most of the coal still needed for the power stations is imported.

That year of the strike, for me, was the highlight of my life. The daily *News Line*, for which I worked, had one reporter and a photographer in the coal fields for the duration. I spent a large part of the year with my camera in Yorkshire and Nottinghamshire following every aspect of the strike. Because we reported the strike from the miners' point of view, we became recognised and trusted by them. We were partisan in that we saw the strike as progressive and necessary, but we never distorted the coverage. On one occasion we arrived at Cresswell pit in Derbyshire at 6.00 a.m. to find about 4,000 pickets were already there – and not a policeman in sight. The miners had closed the pit, and the scene remained peaceful, almost serene, until the arrival, an hour later, of Transit vans full of riot police, hundreds and thousands of them. There followed a violent clash, with numerous arrests and injuries, as the police tried to fulfil their orders from above to reopen the gates to the pit so that they could bus in a few 'scabs' and declare the colliery as working. The picture on the previous page, of two young miners shackled to a lamp-post, was taken on that occasion.

Reading Beverley Trounce's *From a Rock to a Hard Place* transported me back to that extraordinary year. The book gives a voice to the miners themselves, from all over the coal fields, 30 years on. Their memories remain vivid, and they speak openly and humorously about the hard times, the worries and the implications of what they did in 1984/5. None of them express regret. They fought for their jobs as members of the NUM in the teeth of a vicious assault by the forces of the state, the media included. They were supported by hundreds of thousands of working people throughout the land, but were let down by the TUC and the Labour leaders who hardly lifted a finger in support. Rightly, they have stayed proud of their memories.

1

BEGINNINGS 'ALL HELL LET LOOSE'

On the morning of 5 March 1984, former steelworker Ian Wroe turned the corner at the end of his street to be met with an astonishing sight. There were lines of police on both sides of the road as far as the eye could see. He recalls:

Looking in either direction all you could see were rows of police. They seemed to stretch to the horizon, two or even three deep in some places. A lot had dogs, and police vans were everywhere. Normal traffic was blocked off. At first I couldn't work out what was going on but somebody told me it was because they were expecting trouble from the striking miners. Looking down the road to see all these police … well, it was surreal.

The focus of all this police attention was the entrance to Cortonwood Colliery in the village of Brampton Bierlow in South Yorkshire. This was the beginning of the 1984/5 Great Miners' Strike, a strike that would become a bitter battle and would last far longer than anyone expected.

That day the area around Cortonwood Colliery became a no man's land with running battles between pickets and police. At one point, in their attempt to escape, pickets swam across a canal and climbed up the opposite bank. From here they ran towards a housing estate, climbed fences and bolted through back gardens. Police with dogs chased after them while local residents looked on in disbelief. One described the scene: 'Flower beds were churned up, bushes were uprooted and fences collapsed. The noise was just

11

Police line the road at Cortonwood Colliery (*courtesy of Rhoda Allen*).

Pickets begin to assemble at Cortonwood (*courtesy of Rhoda Allen*).

terrible. Men yelling at the top of their voices and police dogs barking non-stop. It were like all hell let loose.'

Within a few days the local miners' welfare and social club had become a media control centre where TV cameras, commentators and newspaper reporters gathered. Meanwhile the miners had constructed a 'picket hut' at the entrance to the colliery, using whatever materials they could lay their hands on. Nicknamed 'The Alamo', after the historic US battle of that name, the hut even had its own crude but effective plumbing system.

These huts provided some protection from the elements and were put together at many sites (as were pit camps, later on, which were often run by miners' wives). If a plumber, electrician or other skilled worker could be called upon to help then so much the better. During cold weather discarded oil drums with holes punched in the sides served as braziers. The police often destroyed the huts but new ones were quickly erected.

The events of 5 March were the result of a government announcement that Cortonwood colliery would close within five weeks. This was to be the first of twenty pit closures that year with a loss of 20,000 jobs under

'The Alamo' (*courtesy of Rhoda Allen*).

Inside 'The Alamo' (*courtesy of Rhoda Allen*).

a scheme devised by Prime Minister Margaret Thatcher and her advisor, Ian MacGregor. The government declared these pits to be uneconomical and no longer viable. Opponents, however, insisted that there was another agenda: that of the destruction of the trade union, much hated by Thatcher, the National Union of Mineworkers (NUM).

The miners of Cortonwood were particularly shocked by the imminent closure of their pit because, just a few days previously, they had been told that there were coal supplies which would last for at least another five years. Furthermore there had been recent investment in expensive machinery and equipment, along with eighty miners being brought in from the nearby Elsecar colliery, which had closed down some time before. The decision to shut down Cortonwood seemed completely illogical and nonsensical. Some suspected that Cortonwood was a way of testing the water for the government: if pit-closure plans were to be implemented then Cortonwood might have seemed the safe option to begin with. It had never been viewed as a particularly militant pit and so it was possible that the miners would accept rather than oppose the plans. Most remain convinced, however, that the announcement about closing Cortonwood was deliberately timed to provoke the NUM into facing up to Margaret Thatcher so that battle could commence, for this was to be the final face-off between the miners and the government.

The 1984/5 strike was the culmination of many years of dispute. In 1910 Home Secretary Winston Churchill sent troops with guns into Wales to quell the striking miners of Tonypandy. The year 1912 saw the first national miners' strike in Britain, followed by the 1926 General Strike. Apart from sporadic local strikes an uneasy truce was maintained until 1972 when the NUM went head-to-head with the National Coal Board over low pay. This, and the strike held two years later, resulted in the collapse of the Tory Government under Edward Heath. The miners had successfully managed to block fuel deliveries to the country's power stations, leading to the government being forced to introduce a three-day working week to conserve electricity.

When Margaret Thatcher became prime minister in 1979 one of her main targets was to significantly weaken the NUM in order to eliminate

Pickets at Cortonwood (*courtesy of Rhoda Allen*).

future conflict. She appointed American businessman and former British Steel Corporation chief Ian MacGregor as head of the National Coal Board. He had recently implemented a major reduction of the workforce in the steel industry and NUM president, Arthur Scargill, was certain that MacGregor would deal with the miners in the same way. Scargill predicted:

> I cannot emphasise enough that the Coal Board's ultimate intention is to wipe out half the South Nottinghamshire coalfield, cut the Midlands area by forty per cent, close down half of the Scottish pits, cut the North Western Area's pits by half, close sixty per cent of the collieries in the North East, wipe out half of North Derbyshire, seventy per cent of the pits in South Wales and shut down twenty Yorkshire collieries. No one can now say that he has not been warned.

Naturally the government strongly refuted this and MacGregor even sent out a reassuring letter to the miners, urging them to ignore Scargill. Scargill's words, however, would prove prophetic. Government papers released in January 2014, under the 'thirty-year rule', confirm that plans had been drawn up to instigate a massive pit closure programme throughout the UK.

Battle lines had been drawn. What the miners could not know, however, was that Margaret Thatcher had made careful preparations to avoid a repetition of 1974. These preparations meant that she felt confident enough to challenge and defeat the NUM. The time was right. Many of

Cartoon of Ian MacGregor which appeared in *The Miner* newspaper, depicting what was felt to be his deceitful nature. NACODS refers to the pit deputies' union (*courtesy of the NUM*).

the strategies to be used had been drawn up using the 1977 Ridley plan, a report written by Conservative MP Nicholas Ridley on how to defeat strikes in nationalised industries. Thatcher's chancellor, Nigel Lawson, stated that it was 'like re-arming to face the threat of Hitler'. Police numbers had been hugely increased with officers receiving a substantial pay rise. They were given specialist training and were issued with new equipment for riot control. Coal had been secretly stockpiled and contracts drawn up with haulage firms to transport it in case railway workers decided to take industrial action in support of the strike. Old laws were resurrected and new ones brought in virtually overnight. The miners were set to face the full might of the government.

Yorkshire striking miner, Charlie Cibor, describes how coal was stockpiled at his colliery of Markham Main in the Yorkshire village of Armthorpe:

> We were naïve. We were digging out the coal and we were noticing that the heaps were becoming massive. It never occurred to us that they were soon to be transported to the power stations. Thatcher was using us to bring about our own downfall.

There was another important weapon that could be used against the striking miners: that of the media. Arthur Scargill soon found that he was being demonised by the press. He was portrayed as a bullying dictator, forcing his views onto the miners whereas, in fact, they have always insisted that

Markham Main Colliery (*courtesy of Leslie Phillips*).

decisions were made at rank and file level with Scargill being instructed by them. Margaret Thatcher had developed a good relationship with media magnate Rupert Murdoch. His daily tabloid, the *Sun*, would go on to produce a photo of Scargill, one arm raised, accompanied by a report accusing him of making a Nazi salute. Disgusted print workers refused to handle the photo and that day's edition of the paper instead carried a message from those workers condemning the attempt to besmirch Scargill. The miners themselves, labelled 'Arthur's Army', were portrayed as violent thugs and were famously described as the 'enemy within' by Thatcher. The BBC later admitted that news footage had been reversed so it appeared that miners were attacking mounted police when, in fact, the reverse was true.

After the first skirmish at Cortonwood the NUM and the government realised there would be no going back. Miners at the nearby colliery of Manvers Main had already walked out three weeks previously over changes in their work conditions and it would not be long before industrial action gathered momentum nationwide, leading to one of the most bitter episodes in British industrial history.

The strike spread rapidly across the UK. Yorkshire flying pickets were despatched to other counties and soon a chain reaction was in process as pit after pit came out. The numbers of flying pickets from other areas increased until there was a network across the country. Ex-striking miners still take pride in how quickly and to what extent their own county's collieries came out on strike. 'Not soft, just south', is a phrase associated with the Kent miners and Philip Sutcliffe, of Snowdown Colliery, goes on to elaborate:

Kent miners were solid and joined the strike straight away, just as we'd done in 1972 and 1974. We were also the last to go back, in an attempt to get sacked miners reinstated. Our collieries consisted of Snowdown, Tilmanstone and Betteshanger. Situated in the middle of the 'Garden of England', we were a major industry in the county. Traditionally the Kent collieries were militant because a lot of blacklisted, rebellious miners who'd been sacked in other areas were sent to the newly-established Kent pits. Snowdown, for example, began in 1912 and quickly gained the nickname of 'The Klondyke' because it got a reputation of being the place where all the rough workers arrived from all over the country – just like the place in America. If you listen to the accents of people who still live round here, for example, you won't hear many typical Kentish ones. People have inherited their parents' and grandparents' accents from all over the place. I suppose you could say militancy is in our genes.

The Kent Coal Board was unofficially amalgamated with Leicestershire and we were told by the powers that be to go there. Well we did go but we weren't going to be restricted and so we joined other flying pickets to stand against working miners everywhere, most especially in Nottinghamshire.

'THE REALLY BRAVE ONES'

There were two major problem areas in the East Midlands where the strike was not welcomed. If anyone mentions the Leicestershire or Nottinghamshire miners then they are likely to be met with derision. 'Scabland!' is the most frequent reply. If, however, the *striking* miners of these two counties are mentioned, the response will usually be, 'They were the really brave ones!' This is because the striking miners there defied the majority who rejected the strike and who continued working. Less than a third of the Nottinghamshire miners came out and the working miners there disassociated themselves from the NUM, instead forming a new union, the Union of Democratic Mineworkers (UDM). In Leicestershire only thirty joined the strike and were nicknamed the 'Dirty Thirty', which, originally meant as an insult by working miners, was adopted by the strikers. They are now something of a local legend.

Eric Eaton, chairman of the Nottinghamshire NUM Ex & Retired Miners explains:

> You just couldn't make them see that their jobs were on the line. They wouldn't accept it and instead believed what Thatcher and MacGregor were telling them. It was frustrating not to be able to get through to them. They wanted a ballot whereas we striking miners knew that it was essential to fight these pit closures in order to protect our communities and to ensure there would be jobs for the next generation.

Phil Fitzpatrick, a Yorkshire flying picket, explains:

> What was really frustrating was that, early on, we'd go to join the Notts picket lines and we were beginning to do really well in persuading the working miners to join us. We were talking peaceably with them and reasoning with them. A lot began to consider striking but then the police cracked down

Members of the Nottinghamshire NUM Ex & Retired Miners Association. Eric Eaton is on the back row, second from left (*courtesy of NUM Ex & Retired Miners Association*).

and that was when borders were closed off. They wanted to prevent us from having any communication with the Notts miners.

So what was the reason for these miners refusing to come out on strike? Eric Eaton replies:

> Money. There were differences in pay across the country and Nottinghamshire miners earned a good wage. They also had some of the best working conditions. It was an 'I'm alright, Jack' mentality. They came up with all sorts of excuses but it was just greed. Pure and simple greed. One told me that he couldn't possibly join us because he'd just taken out a new mortgage. Well, so had I. My wife and I had just moved house with a bigger mortgage and then, just a few days later, I was on strike.

The Nottinghamshire and Leicestershire collieries were considered to be conservative and non-militant. They remained influenced by the

Twenty-fifth anniversary congratulations sent to the Nottinghamshire striking miners from the NUM headquarters, Barnsley (*courtesy of the NUM*).

The Yorkshire Area of the NUM sends fraternal greetings to all Nottingham NUM members past and present, who took part in the historic struggle of 1984/85.

As we reach this landmark anniversary we salute the loyalty shown by the Nottinghamshire Area NUM and the resolve displayed in fighting for their Union, their communities and their jobs.

We can only admire your resolve given the circumstances you found yourselves in, in Nottinghamshire.

HISTORY WILL CONFIRM THE CAUSE WAS JUST AND REMAINS SO TODAY.

doctrine of 'Spencerism', based on the actions of Nottinghamshire miners' leader, George Spencer, who, during the Great Strike of 1926, formed an independent union after collaborating with mine-owners. Although both counties' miners eventually became NUM members, they insisted on holding a ballot to determine whether their region should take industrial action. This was frustrating for the striking miners who considered ballots to be divisive, believing that it was essential for the workforce to unite nationally to keep the collieries open.

When the strike began, Kent miners travelled to Bagworth pit in Leicestershire to spread the word and encourage the Leicestershire miners to take action. The miners there agreed to take part but the majority soon returned to work after being instructed to do so by Jack Jones, the moderate local NUM official. Darren Moore, a member of the 'Dirty Thirty', says that he felt 'demoralised and disappointed' to find that his colleagues had abandoned the strike. By now the Kent pickets had gone

Leaflet supporting the 'Dirty Thirty'.

elsewhere, assuming they had been successful in Leicestershire. Pickets from South Wales arrived and Darren, aged 24, had to explain to them what had happened. The Welsh miners, he says:

> … could not understand why the men are crossing the picket line because their tradition was, if there's a picket line, you don't cross it.
>
> The Leicestershire railwaymen refused to transport the coal and they became an integral part of the strike. We were so grateful to them and to us it

Role of honour: members of the 'Dirty Thirty'.

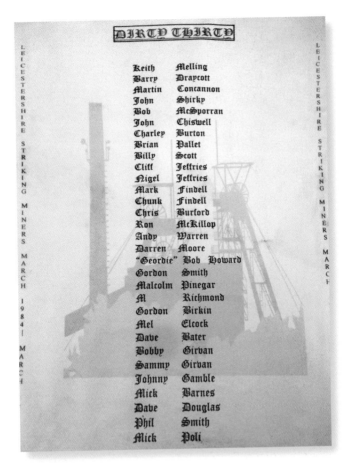

Leaflet supporting the 'Dirty Thirty'.

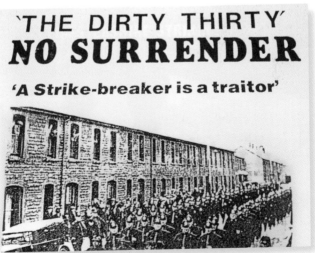

seemed crazy that another union was giving us more support than our own. On one occasion I heard a union official tell one of the scabs, 'Sneak in at the bottom gate and then you won't have to cross the picket line.' Unbelievable! This was our so-called union!

Those of us who were on strike were not only losing our wages but were also compromising our future. One miner who came out was near to retirement and he risked losing his pension. He was a brave man who could see that there would be no jobs for the next generation unless we took action. I myself gave up the chance of promotion. I was training to be a pit deputy when I went on strike but knew I'd never be able to get that job now because I'd annoyed too many people.

Elsewhere in the country, however, the strike was taking hold and battle had commenced between the miners and the government. Very soon this would become war.

2

BROTHERS IN ARMS

I'd managed to dodge the police and get over the border from Yorkshire into Nottinghamshire. Those lads needed all the help they could get. I reached a picket line and the Notts lads were right glad to see me. They invited me into their hut. There were women and children in there as well as miners. They didn't have much but they shared their food wi' me. It was a humbling experience. I would've died for them that day, and that's the truth.

Bruce Wilson, Silverwood Colliery, Yorkshire

In 1984 spring had arrived and there was excitement in the air. The striking miners were in jubilant mood and felt confident that this would be an intense but short-lived battle resulting in victory for them. The government, however, was equally confident. Both sides would be shocked at what was to come. Thousands of people across the country would soon be embroiled in what was virtually a civil war lasting for almost a year.

End of a day's picketing (*courtesy of Bruce Wilson*).

The miners were unprepared for the new government tactics which were about to be unleashed upon them. They did, however, have a powerful weapon of their own: the government had totally underestimated the loyalties and strong bonds which had formed amongst the striking miners. These men were not acting out of individual self-interest but instead worked to protect one another and would look out for one another.

The nature of the job meant that strong friendships were built up between coal miners, especially if they worked underground as opposed to working on the pit-top.

Accidents, often fatal, were commonplace below ground and nearly every miner has a story to tell of injury and death. Yorkshire miner Tom Lindsay's voice still breaks as he describes the death of a friend who got caught in some machinery:

> It were so hot down there that we used to just strip off, see. Well, this lad got trapped in some machinery. We were desperately trying to grab hold of him before he got more caught but the sweat from his body meant we just couldn't get a grip on him and it were like he were swallowed up. That were forty year ago and I still think on it.

Clipstone pickets, Nottinghamshire, with some of their children. Children were often allowed to play close to, or even on, the picket line if it was thought safe enough (*courtesy of Doug Broadfoot*).

Police requisition a local resident's garden near Harworth Colliery, Nottinghamshire (*courtesy of Bruce Wilson*).

Another tells of how he drifted in and out of consciousness as he lay trapped underground for several hours after a tunnel collapsed:

> The rescue team could see my hand and lower bit of my arm sticking out the rubble. They kept trying to pull me but they didn't realise that the rest of my arm and my shoulder were well and truly trapped. I was in agony every time they pulled. I tried to shout to them to stop but they couldn't hear. I ended up with a broken collarbone and a dislocated elbow but, to be honest, I thought I was going to die.

Many miners describe their colleagues below ground as 'one big family', always watching out for each another and, more often than not, prepared to take risks to help one another. 'We were like brothers and, when the strike was on, we became brothers in arms. All for one, one for all.'

The comradeship formed underground became even stronger above ground during the strike. Many new friendships were also formed. Charlie Cibor describes how, before the strike, it had been the Saturday night custom of local pit-village lads to challenge those from other villages. There would be drinking followed by fighting, perhaps over girls, and a good time was had by all. The old enmities were forgotten during the strike, however, and these new friendships remained strong afterwards. It no longer mattered which village or which pit you came from, or even which county, for, as striking Nottinghamshire miner Eric Eaton says, 'If you were one of t'lads, then that's all that mattered.'

27

Durham picket, Norman Strike ('Yes – that really is my name', he sighs) describes how, at first, the relationship between pickets and police could sometimes be quite jovial, with good-natured insults and catcalls being traded. Rows of police would stand opposite picket lines and there would be 'a lot of pushing and shoving' as the two front lines converged. At this point it seemed to many like a 'phoney strike', just as there had been the so-called 'phoney war' in 1939 Britain. Some of the miners had friends and relations within the local police force. In such cases agreements were often made beforehand that, if a picket were to find himself opposite a friend, relation or neighbour, then one of them would move down the lines to stand elsewhere. The government soon wised up to this situation, however, realising that to use police officers to stand against their own communities was a mistake. So the game changed and officers were brought in from different counties. It seems that each police force gained its own reputation. Nottinghamshire police, for example, were considered by many to be one of the worst and most ruthless.

The early jubilation felt amongst the striking miners was soon dispelled. The mood changed into one of grief and shock when, on 15 March David Jones, a 23-year-old Yorkshire striking miner, was killed in the Nottinghamshire village of Ollerton by a brick being thrown at pickets.

Charlie Cibor, along with several other pickets, had been arrested there and spent the night in jail:

Police and pickets at Cortonwood (*courtesy of Rhoda Allen*).

Early next morning this copper came and unlocked the cell doors. He told us to go. This was strange because we thought we were going to be charged with summat but he just told us to clear off. He was very quiet and it seemed a bit strange so we asked him what was going on. He told us a picket, a young lad, had been killed. We were that shocked. We just couldn't believe it.

David Jones' funeral, held on 23 March, was attended by more than 3,000 people with over thirty pits represented. There would be another fatality in June when Joe Green from Kellingley Colliery in Yorkshire was crushed by a lorry while on picket duty at Ferrybridge Power Station.

The violence which had erupted at Ollerton was because 8,000 police from combined forces had been sent in to patrol the Nottinghamshire border in an attempt to prevent Yorkshire flying pickets from crossing over. The government was determined not to allow any dialogue between the Yorkshire pickets and the Nottinghamshire miners. When the pickets reached Ollerton they were confronted by lines of police barring their entry to the village and a battle began which continued for hours.

For the miners, these border controls were not just about trying to separate pickets. For them they were also a symbol of tyranny. Many felt outraged that, despite their fathers and grandfathers having fought in two world wars, they were now being denied the basic freedom of being allowed to travel around their own country. For them this had become a civil liberties issue and they

The parents of David Jones present his portrait to Arthur Scargill (*courtesy of the NUM*).

refused to back down. This feeling was echoed everywhere. In Kent, flying pickets were being blocked from using the Dartford Tunnel to prevent them travelling to the Midlands and North. Police patrolling the tunnel entrance would stop any run-down looking car carrying three or four male passengers. Kent miner Phillip Sutcliffe describes the anger and humiliation felt by many:

> My father and my forefathers had fought for this country and yet I was being treated like a criminal just for wanting to move around freely. I'd done nothing wrong and never been in any trouble. We couldn't believe how we were being treated. Anyway, after a while the police gave up trying to patrol the tunnel because we'd just drive round it and get to where we wanted in the end, following a different direction. It was a pointless exercise.

The government now upped the ante in its attempt to defeat the miners. New measures were brought in. Drivers were turned back under threat of arrest on roads in mining areas and police were allowed to impose curfews and identity checks throughout Nottinghamshire. A desperate game of cat and mouse had begun, with the pickets often surviving on their wits alone. The ability to keep one step ahead was paramount. Bruce Wilson explains:

> It was easier for us to confuse the police than the other way round because we were better at thinking on our feet. We'd always had to do that down the pit because dangerous situations would suddenly arise and you had to act quick, like. The bobbies, though, well they were just used to obeying orders. A lot of them weren't used to thinking for themselves. Summat would crop up and you could tell they didn't know what to do because there was no one there to shout orders to them. We used to have fun playing tricks on 'em and watching their faces when they realised they'd messed up. They'd be running round like headless chickens. Sometimes it were like summat out of Keystone Cops. A right laugh.

A new breed of police officer arrived on the scene, however. The dreaded 'Met' (Metropolitan Police) were, according to one picket, '... more like robots than people. They just didn't care about what they did to you. They just wanted to get you. There were nowt human about them.'

'You could always tell it were the Met,' explains another, 'they wore a particular type of white shirt. They behaved differently. You wouldn't want to mess with them.'

Pickets also had to contend with the infamous 'snatch squads', who would, quite literally, snatch anyone they could get hold of. Wearing yellow high-visibility jackets, they would often stand behind the front row of a police line. Pickets became wary of getting too close to the line in the knowledge that a member of the snatch squad might suddenly dash out, grab them and dispatch them off to colleagues waiting by the police vans. Snatch squads were meant to aim at ringleaders but many pickets learned not to make eye contact with any of them as this was sometimes seen as provocative behaviour.

'They were usually big buggers, an' all,' recalls Bruce Wilson. 'They'd be about six foot four tall. It were difficult to break free from them once you'd been snatched.'

A typical confrontational situation would be where perhaps ten rows of police in riot gear would stand some way apart from the picket lines. The police had got into the habit of banging their shields loudly as a form of intimidation.

'Everybody had watched that film *Zulu*,' Norman Strike explains, 'and those police banging on their shields reminded us of it. So we'd all shout "Zuluuu" … and we'd charge. It spread from pit to pit so that soon everybody was doing it. It was a bit of a laugh but we were also serious. Hearing those police banging with full force on their shields made you feel threatened and we needed a way to retaliate.'

The 'pushing and shoving' could be life-threatening to both pickets and police if they were in the front rows. The force from the men behind could prove lethal if anyone fell.

'Snatch squad' at Harworth (*courtesy of Bruce Wilson*).

Bruce:

I was in the front row and suddenly found my face pushed right up against this copper's face. It were almost like we were kissing ... I don't know who thought it were worse, me or him! I can laugh now, looking back, but at the time I thought I was going to be killed. I could feel I was being pushed down onto the ground and I couldn't breathe. Terrifying.

Phil Fitzpatrick:

The police would surround a group of us and it would become like a rugby scrum. Once they backed off there'd be helmets, truncheons, whatever, all over the ground. Once I got home to find a copper's glove had become wedged inside my coat.

As with any battle, both sides were constantly devising new ways to outwit the enemy. Groups of pickets would form a wedge shape and charge into police lines. Meanwhile the police became adept at using a pincer movement to surround the pickets. At night, or during the dark hours of an early winter's morning, police would stealthily creep through any nearby woods to reach the pickets, sometimes even hiding in trees to wait for the enemy to appear. ('Ay up! The Special Branch have arrived!' became a long-standing joke.)

'It did get creepy in the dark when you couldn't see them ...', says Charlie Cibor, '... so we'd start a fire because in that way you could see their helmets gleaming.'

Police and pickets at Cresswell, Derbyshire (*courtesy of Bruce Wilson*).

Sometimes, however, there were no helmets: police would dispense with their usual uniform and would instead wear dark-coloured boiler suits for camouflage.

Bruce:

> We were making our way through some woods one night trying to be as quiet as we could. We were pretty sure the police were in there somewhere. They'd started wearing very dark-blue boiler suits and balaclavas so they couldn't be seen. My mate goes, 'Ay up ... look over there, I can see rabbits' eyes shining in the dark. They look bloody big rabbits!' ... so I looked. I whispered to him, 'They're not rabbits, you daft bugger, they're f–ing police dogs!'

Humour was part and parcel of the picket line; some of it black, some pure farce.

Cyril Brazier, a Kent miner from Snowdown Colliery, describes how police came searching for him and his friends who were on picket duty in the Midlands:

> We'd been sent to picket in Leicestershire and we were staying at a farmhouse somewhere. We always stayed somewhere out of the way because if the scabs found us, we'd be attacked. Sometimes there'd even be police helicopters looking for striking miners. This farmer was sympathetic towards the strike. It was a winter's day and bitterly cold. We got up early and got ready to drive to the picket line but the car was completely frosted over. Everything was iced up and we couldn't get the engine going. We'd been out there for ages trying to fix it when some coppers arrived. We recognised them from the day before when we'd been on the picket line. They'd been beating us wi' their truncheons. Our hearts sank. They asked us what we were doing and we said, 'What do you think we're bloody well doing? We're trying to get the bloody car to start! Anyway, what are YOU doing?'
>
> 'Well', one of 'em replied, 'when you didn't show up on the picket line this morning we decided to come and see if you needed a lift.' They were quite serious. I told 'em to clear off so they did. Once we got back to the picket line it was business as usual.

Another miner tells of the time he was attacked by the mother of a young picket:

Pickets and their families march behind the Darfield Main banner, South Yorkshire (*courtesy of Graham Reeves*).

Her son had arrived home black and blue after his first day on the picket line. I think he was only about 16. She was furious. She came looking for me and found me in the welfare club with my mates. She was yelling that I hadn't looked after her boy and started whacking me with her brolly. Bloody hell, she was terrifying! We should've got her on the picket line with us! Her lad never came again – she wouldn't let him out.

Pickets weren't averse to playing tricks on one another, as Bruce Wilson recalls:

I was usually the driver when we tried to cross the border from Yorkshire into Nottinghamshire. The other lads would crouch down in the back of the car so they wouldn't be seen. There's no way the police would let you through if there was more than one of you. Sometimes we'd come to a road block and I'd just put my foot down and run through it. Seconds later a jam-sandwich (police car) would be after you. On one occasion we were chased but the police finally gave up and left us alone. I wasn't going to tell the lads that though. They were still crouched down in the back and practically screaming with terror because I was going so fast. I kept this up for some time and you can imagine the reaction I got when they realised what I'd been doing.

Charlie Cibor describes how he and his mates learned to go picketing armed with packets of chocolate biscuits:

> You'd be standing in the front row opposite lines of police with dogs. They'd come at you with these big Alsations snarling and growling. So we'd chuck chocolate biscuits at the dogs who gobbled them up and became friendly. The police would get really mad at this and try to make the dogs leave the biscuits alone and attack us. All that happened was that the dogs would start barking at the police and try to attack them instead. It made the police furious and they'd have to turn round and walk away with the dogs pulling on their leads trying to get back to us for more biscuits.

On the whole, though, picket-line duty was a serious business and the threat of injury was always present. Two were killed, many were hospitalised and finished up in intensive care. Bruce Wilson: 'The longer the strike went on, the more determined the government became. The police were now becoming like a paramilitary unit. It was at Orgreave coking plant, near Rotherham, that police first used riot gear against the pickets.' It was here, on 18 June, that violence would escalate to such a pitch that the 'Battle of Orgreave' would become a defining moment of the strike.

Silverwood (Yorks) pickets, Granville Richardson (NUM Branch President), Ian Evers and Bruce Wilson (2014).

Silverwood
picket Bob Taylor
(2014).

Silverwood
picket Terry
Cassidy (2014).

3

SOMETIMES IT ALL JUST GOT TOO MUCH

Orgreave coking plant had become a strategic location in the battle between the government and the striking miners. On becoming Prime Minister one of Margaret Thatcher's main priorities had been to stockpile coal at the nation's power stations. It was lack of coal at these which had been a major factor in the miners' success during the 1972 and 1974 strikes. Now, with the power stations well equipped, the striking miners turned their attention to the steelworks, which were vulnerable because they were dependent on supplies coming in from the coking plants. During March, production at some steel works had been deliberately reduced in order not to exhaust coal supplies. At the end of April railway unions backed up the miners by refusing to transport more than one daily train-load of coke to Ravenscraig Steel Works in Scotland. Lorry convoys were requisitioned to take it, leading to clashes with police as pickets tried to persuade drivers to turn back.

Orgreave was the first time police used riot gear in an industrial dispute in the UK (*courtesy of Bruce Wilson*).

A similar situation occurred when rail unions declared their solidarity with the miners by refusing to carry coke to the Scunthorpe Steel Works in Lincolnshire. The government turned to the haulage firms which had been put on standby for such an eventuality, and lorries were brought in to deliver coking coal from Orgreave, with pickets attempting to halt the proceedings. Things had been markedly different back in the 1970s when drivers had refused to cross picket lines. This time around, however, many of them were no longer unionised and were eager to cash in on the high wages offered. As they drove into and out of the steel works, protected by banks of police, some would gleefully wave banknotes at the pickets. Working man had been set against working man. The old adage of 'divide and rule' had been well and truly put into practice.

Picketing went on for several weeks at Orgreave although, much to the disappointment of its rank and file members, NUM area leaders refused to call for mass picketing there for more than two days at a time. This lack of support from their union would leave striking miners at the site dangerously vulnerable.

Ian Metcalfe, of Markham Colliery, Derbyshire, was a flying picket at Orgreave:

Orgreave coking station, June 1984 (*courtesy of Bruce Wilson*).

We'd be looking across the fields towards the motorway. We'd see the traffic stop and we knew what was coming. The lorries were arriving surrounded by a massive police escort. Our job was to try to stop the lorry drivers, which would mean battling with the police.

Dozens of pickets were arrested on 29 May. Arthur Scargill publicly condemned the police for their use of riot gear and horses. He himself was arrested at Orgreave the next day. Thatcher announced that here was 'an attempt to substitute the rule of the mob for the rule of law, and it must not succeed'.

There were increasingly violent episodes at what has become known as the 'Battle of Orgreave', the culmination of these being on 18 June when 5,000 pickets were met with 4,500 police officers in riot gear, many on horseback and others with dogs. Looking back, many have commented that the beautiful, warm summer's day was so completely at odds with the darkness of the scenes to come. There are photos of pickets, lying, seemingly carelessly, hands behind their heads, in the fields around Orgreave. Long, dark, dense rows of riot police are positioned between them and the coking plant. Many pickets, in fact, were feeling uneasy that the police had been so unusually helpful that morning, even to the point of helping them find parking spaces. Could it be that they had been been set up? ... and, if so, for what?

Ian Metcalfe:

There were lines and lines of police in riot gear at the other end of the field. Suddenly, to our amazement, the lines parted and police on horseback came charging through. We couldn't believe it. We threw anything at them we could get our hands on but it was useless. We started running as fast as we could. We ran and half fell down an embankment.

Norman Strike describes how pickets were stunned when they realised that officers on horseback were lunging in full charge towards them:

You could feel the galloping of the horses' hooves. It was like the ground was shaking. We turned to run and it was terrifying to feel the horses getting closer and closer. We knew the police would show no mercy. As the horse got nearer you could hear the swishing noise of the truncheon as an officer tried to hit you. I managed to leap over an embankment onto some ground below. Others weren't so lucky. We were wearing jeans, T-shirts and trainers against

Police charging at Orgreave (*courtesy of Peter Arkell*).

police in full riot gear with weapons and on horseback. We didn't stand a chance.

I remember I kept shouting to the police, 'Why are you doing this? We're just coal miners! Ordinary miners!'

Ian recalls that 'About thirty of us took cover in a nearby supermarket but the police very quickly surrounded the building and had us trapped. The supermarket manager hid us in storerooms until they gave up and left.'

By all accounts, individual men were screaming as they were set upon by two, three or more police officers. Some of these scenes are available on video footage, filmed by photographers who had placed themselves in the middle of the battle. Men were crying and some were vomiting with pain. There were elderly men who, unable to run, collapsed and were half carried, half dragged by the younger ones. Many of the fleeing pickets genuinely feared for their lives. Eventually some were awarded a total of almost £500,000 in compensation for assault, unlawful arrest and malicious prosecution. The trials of those arrested collapsed when it was discovered that police officers had made use of unreliable evidence. A BBC TV documentary claiming that officers had

Orgreave with riot police in the background (*courtesy of Peter Arkell*).

doctored statements resulted in the investigation of South Yorkshire Police by the Independent Police Claims Commission. In 1991 the BBC itself issued an apology when it admitted that film footage of mounted police charging into pickets had, in fact, been reversed, giving the impression that pickets had attacked police. The precise nature of the events that unfolded that day is still a subject of debate with a formal IPCC investigation under consideration.

On that day there were twice as many pickets injured as police, with many hospitalised, including Arthur Scargill. This episode had redefined the perimeters of the strike. After Orgreave, pickets took with them the unspoken message that, from now on, almost anything would be acceptable in terms of beating the enemy. Miners and their families had always believed that the strike was an act of self-defence against an attack on them and their communities. Orgreave strengthened that belief.

Paul Winter of Dodworth Colliery, Yorkshire and then later Grimethorpe, describes a sight he has never been able to forget:

I noticed a picket standing alone in a nearby field. What struck me was that he was standing so still and had his arms somehow wrapped around his head.

41

It was as if he was trying to block out all the sights and sounds. There was a wet patch in the crotch of his jeans. He was so frightened that he'd pissed his s'en. Completely and utterly humiliated.

Many left that place on that day traumatised. I personally couldn't face the picket line at all for a few weeks. I couldn't go back straight away. Sometimes it all just got too much.

The NUM called off any future picketing at Orgreave but there were those who continued. At this point, women's groups, appalled at what had happened, felt they had to make a stand by setting up their own picket lines and pit camps there. The riot police continued to patrol. Two sides, watching one another and waiting for any sign of hostile action. There was now a different, almost funereal atmosphere. The miners knew there was no chance of victory at this site and many criticised their union, feeling that it had not been supportive enough. It was felt that if the NUM had organised mass daily picketing there then this would have spurred on other unions to support them. As it was, the striking miners felt a bitter disappointment that there had been no display of solidarity from other workers, especially as they themselves had always offered support to other unions. There was some encouragement when, later that month, 50,000 people joined marches and demonstrations in support of the strike. Some rail workers took strike action for a day and many teachers followed suit. On the whole, though, the miners felt abandoned. Their resolve, however, strengthened. There would be no backing down.

4

NO HOLDS BARRED

The government was spending what would become millions on policing the strike and Margaret Thatcher was not going to allow this money to have been spent in vain. Tougher measurements were brought in by the government meaning that the striking miners needed an increasing amount of subterfuge and guile to get across county borders. Pickets' cars were being stopped and turned back even though, often, they were miles away from any colliery. The miners retaliated by deliberately blocking motorways, causing, on one occasion, a 9-mile tailback. Sympathetic lorry drivers used CB radio to urge their colleagues to join in and car drivers handed out supplies to the pickets. Charlie Cibor remembers how he and others, sitting on the grassy banks along the M1, watched as furious police officers began to smash car windscreens:

> They weren't sure who were pickets and who were civilians so they just started randomly smashing everybody's. A lot of ordinary drivers were on our

Pickets stop traffic on the M180 near Scunthorpe (*courtesy of Bruce Wilson*).

side, anyway, and had been handing out drinks, snacks and packets of fags. We started shouting, 'Hooligans! You're all hooligans!' at the police, which made them even more angry.

Bruce Wilson adds, 'We were chatting with drivers and found that many of them supported us. They were giving us drinks and biscuits. Somebody started a game of football further down the road and we all joined in.'

Yorkshire picket from Woolley Colliery, Phil Fitzpatrick, tells how desperate this game of one-upmanship was becoming:

We were on our way to a big meeting in Mansfield. Police were everywhere as they were expecting trouble and they were stopping pickets' cars on the A38. About twenty-five of us abandoned our cars and decided to walk across the fields to Mansfield. A few cops caught up with us ordering us to turn back which, of course, we refused to do. They kept following us and in the end we turned to them and told them if they wanted a fight we would give them one. They said they didn't want any confrontation and that they'd escort us to town to make sure we caused no trouble. We told them there would be no trouble as we were just on our way to a meeting, not to a picket line. They went on and on about escorting us so we just shrugged our shoulders and agreed. We went back to the roadside and continued walking

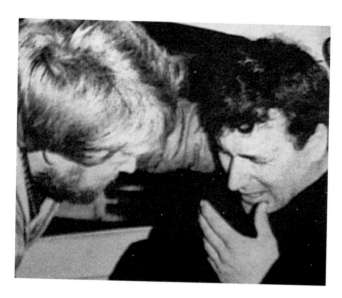

A friend helps an injured picket who has glass splinters in his eye after police smash the car windscreen at Brodsworth Colliery, South Yorkshire (*courtesy of the NUM*).

Police reinforcements arrive at Cadley Hill Colliery, Derbyshire (*courtesy of Bruce Wilson*).

into town with what by now was a big group of police surrounding us. Then we noticed we were being passed on the road by a whole load of police cars and vans heading for Mansfield. We began to feel uneasy, suspecting that we'd been set up. Sure enough, on reaching the outskirts of the town, we were ambushed by dozens of police … Some of us escaped and I managed to roll out of the way, under a privet hedge. It was terrifying and I still have flashbacks whenever I travel along that road.

Badges, that was another thing. If they saw you wearing a badge of any sort they'd want to know what it was for. I'd been to a gig one night with my mates. Next day I was walking round a village in Nottinghamshire looking for somewhere to buy food. There were police patrolling about everywhere as usual. I'd bought a badge of the band I'd been to see and pinned it on my T-shirt. This copper grabs me and demands to know what it was. Was it to do with the strike? I told him no, it was a band and I'd just been to see them. It seems almost funny now but in those days I felt like I was living in a police state.

Jenny Metcalfe of the Derbyshire Women's Support Group and wife of Derbyshire striking miner, Ian:

> When you were about to cross a county border you had to remember to take your badges off. As soon as the police saw those badges they had you marked as a picket. We all, men and women, would remove our badges when trying to pass ourselves off as ordinary citizens and then, if we made it over the border, we'd pin them back on again.

Joyce Sheppard of Yorkshire Women Against Pit Closures, continues:

> Badges were important to us because, like pit banners, they were a way of proclaiming solidarity with one another. We didn't have a uniform like the police did but our badges showed who we were and what we were fighting for. We'd have a badge for our pit, a badge to say where you'd been picketing and badges were made to mark important events. Sometimes, on a picket line, it would be a bit like a school playground because we'd all be admiring one another's badges and swapping and trading them ... makes me smile when I think of that.

Hatred of the enemy was increasing on both sides and the miners began to suspect that the police were now using 'dirty' tactics. 'We were pretty sure our phones were being tapped', says one striking miner:

> You would hear a 'click' whenever you went to make a call or receive one. For a long time we hadn't been able to understand how, when we turned up at a picket line, there were always loads of police already there, waiting for us. We became suspicious of one another – was somebody acting as an informer? But pickets all over the country were saying the same thing ... 'The police are listening in to our phone calls.'
>
> Anyway we realised that we'd have to speak in code. Each colliery was given a number and when we were arranging to go picketing that's what we'd use. We soon found that masses of police weren't ready and waiting for us anymore when we got to a particular picket line. One of the biggest mistakes had been to let the police know how many of us would be at Orgreave.

By now there was a network of flying pickets and women's support groups spreading across the country. Police, under pressure from Thatcher and

Harworth Colliery (*courtesy of Bruce Wilson*).

MacGregor, were stepping up their efforts to prevent the crossing of county borders. Random arrests were increasing as police tried to gain control of the situation.

'It got really crazy,' says Tom Lindsay. 'Half the time you couldn't understand what you were being charged with. Some were charged with summat called "violence against persons unknown". Well to me that seems ridiculous. If it was a person unknown then how could that person make a complaint to the police?'

'When you got arrested they'd take your photo' says Charlie Cibor. 'Well that was illegal and I told them so. They carried on so you'd try to cover your face with your hands but it was difficult because you'd been handcuffed. They wanted photos so they could circulate them to warn one another who to look out for.'

A Kent miner remembers being arrested and taken off to the police van. 'When I asked the copper why I was being arrested he replied, "Don't worry, I'll think of something".'

Jenny Metcalfe was incensed when she saw a young picket being taken away for no apparent reason:

> He was just a young lad. They started hitting him. I'd been standing near him on the picket line and I can honestly say he hadn't caused any trouble. The police grabbed him and took him. I decided to offer myself as a witness to vouch for his good behaviour. It didn't help him though.

Groups of miners would be given their instructions on a daily basis about where to picket. Bruce Wilson recounts how every evening he and the other pickets would go to their local miners' welfare club to collect their orders for next day.

'Not a word was spoken,' he says. 'You just walked up to the table to collect the bit of paper with your instructions on. I was always the driver for my lot so I was given a small amount of money for petrol. The police would always try to arrest the driver because that meant the other lads in the car would often have to walk home.'

Each group had a designated 'bell man' who would rouse sleeping pickets in case an emergency situation arose. Pickets would often also elect

Anger at Cresswell as a picket is arrested (*courtesy of Bruce Wilson*).

someone who, at the end of the day, would go around searching for and collecting those who had become isolated for one reason or another. This was not always an easy task as some had been arrested while others could be in hospital. In a pre-mobile phone society it was an especially difficult and time-consuming job trying to track people down. Furthermore it had become increasingly common to take arrested pickets to jails away from their local area. They would be isolated from one another and not allowed to make contact with their families who were often distraught with worry.

'They took me miles away to Paddington Green in London', says one Yorkshire picket. 'That's where terrorists are held. There were some IRA guys being held there. I was being treated like a terrorist. It was three days before my family found out where I was.'

Tom Lindsay:

They took me once and I was gone for days. I hadn't been able to get a message to my family or anyone. They all thought I'd gone off to picket somewhere else in the country. Don't forget we had no mobile phones or Internet in them days.

Norman Strike:

Just because we'd had to be tough on the picket lines didn't mean we weren't afraid of ending up in jail. It scared us. Not only would we have a criminal record which would affect our job prospects but we were also scared of some of the people we'd be put with. Real hardened criminals.

Often a group of you would be arrested and let out on bail if you agreed not to go anywhere near a colliery or picket line. Of course we'd all agree, get let go ... then straight back to the picket lines. One judge got sick of seeing me. The other lads were charged, sentenced and released. I was kept back. I couldn't understand what was going on. I was given two weeks in jail and I was gob-smacked. They took me down and put me with this massive, shaven-headed Scotsman with 'EVIL' tattooed on his forehead. I was shitting myself. He came up to me and put his face right in mine. 'I've killed three people', he whispered, '... what you in here for?' I gulped and told him I was a striking miner. He stepped back ... 'You're a what?' he shouted. I told him again, 'I'm a striking miner.'

He stared at me. 'Good God!' he said, 'What's this country coming to when they put striking miners in with people like me!'

Nottinghamshire miner Bob Collier of Newstead was put in a cell with what seemed to be a member of a religious sect:

> He wasn't in prison uniform yet but looked like he was wearing some sort of tunic and was wearing those flat sandals. He'd shaved his head and had peace symbols painted on his face. He was sitting cross-legged on the floor with his eyes closed and was chanting. Well, there was I, straight from the picket lines, my face all bloodied. I was bruised and aching all over. I'd just about

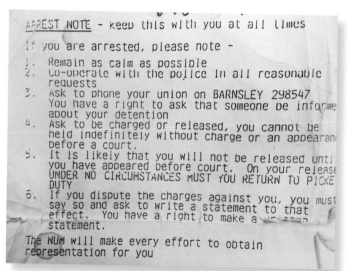

Arrest guidelines issued to pickets by the NUM (reproduced with permission of Barnsley Archives & Local Studies).

One of several arrest notes issued to Derbyshire picket Ian Metcalfe.

had enough that day. I chose the best bunk and I said to this guy, 'Right, I'm having this one!' Well, he stood up and he was massive. Great big bloke. 'I'm in here for grievous bodily harm', he said, looking as if he wanted to kill me. 'As a matter of fact I really hurt someone. I mean really hurt them.' He came closer to me and said, 'I choose the bunk. Do you understand?' I swallowed and nodded. I hardly dared go to sleep that night. I laugh about it now but I was scared back then, I can tell you.

Fortunately for the arrested pickets there was a group of sympathetic lawyers who would often turn up and arrange for the miners' release. Some of these lawyers are still working today in an attempt to win justice for miners who were sacked as a result of their actions on the picket line. Ian Metcalfe was arrested more than once and his MP, Tony Benn, intervened. Meanwhile the Orgreave Truth and Justice Campaign has been organised by former NCB administrative worker and picket, Barbara Jackson.

Beatings and arrests continued. Charlie Cibor describes the pain of being 'truncheoned':

> They would use these new 'bendy' truncheons. They were longer than normal truncheons and had a kind of inbuilt spring so that when you were hit by one, it would kind of wrap itself around you. A bit like a metal whip. They really hurt and I'd see lads curled up on the ground, crying with pain.

'Another tactic', says Norman Strike, 'was for the police to chuck a truncheon at you if they couldn't catch you. You'd get hit and you'd instinctively stop to put your hand on the pain. That's when you got caught.'

Riot police at Silverwood Colliery (*courtesy of Bruce Wilson*).

Pickets were constantly devising new ways to beat the police and some pits gained a reputation for being more militant than others. Young David Ayrton arrived at the picket line outside Markham Main Colliery in Armthorpe, Yorkshire. Not a miner, he had been a railway worker and factory worker, but by 1984 he had been unemployed for three years:

> There had been huge industrial decline in the area with massive unemployment in Doncaster. I felt I had to join the striking miners to make a stand about the situation. I was 24 years old and had already been arrested while on picket lines for other industries. I was more experienced than a lot of lads my age. Nevertheless when I arrived in Armthorpe I found I was so frightened that I was shaking. Some of the other pickets laughed but promised they'd look after me. I knew that Armthorpe had a reputation. I knew there was going to be more violence here than at a lot of other pits. All the pickets were brave there but, from what I saw, I would say that Charlie Cibor was the bravest. He put his arm round me when he saw I was shaking. He laughed but told me I'd be okay and that he and the others would watch out for me. He took risks that no one else would have dared take. He inspired others. He was constantly being arrested but always came back to carry on.

Riot police patrolling a Yorkshire pit-village (*courtesy of Peter Arkell*).

At one point the situation in Armthorpe became so out of control that, as with Ollerton in Nottinghamshire, police stormed the village and completely surrounded it, isolating it from the surrounding area. Pickets had somehow managed to requisition a bulldozer and other heavy vehicles, which they positioned to block the arrival of buses of working miners and police. Tyres were set alight and the air was full of thick black smoke. A battle ensued between pickets and police with one witness reporting, 'There were so many rocks and bricks being thrown that it was like the sky went black.'

Pandemonium ensued. Residents hid inside while police in riot gear charged through gardens and kicked open front doors in a bid to find the ringleaders. Groups of police hid from sight, ready to ambush pickets running by. Some of the older striking miners withdrew, not wishing to be involved at this level. One explained:

> The young lads were having a field day and I mean police as well as miners. I saw police officers bunched up together behind a bush at the end of my path. It was like they were in a rugby scrum. Laughing away, they were, waiting to ambush pickets. We older ones just felt we couldn't take it that far. We were family men with young kids. We had responsibilities for our families. A lot of the young ones weren't married and had no one but themselves to worry about.

Flying pickets arriving in Armthorpe the next day were amazed to find what now resembled '… a battle-scene in Beirut, like we were always seeing on the news'. Front doors were hanging off, windows had been smashed and small fires were still burning.

Many striking miners talk about the time they 'snapped'. For many it was Orgreave but there were other incidents when men (and women) felt pushed to the point where the rule of law no longer seemed relevant. Looking back, many are amazed at their behaviour, barely able to recognise their younger selves. 'I can't believe I did that!' is a common refrain.

For months the battles raged on between pickets and police. The government continued to devise new strategies to defeat the miners while the media relentlessly portrayed them as thugs and 'scum'. The government, the police and the media were not the only enemies, however. The miners had their own 'enemy within'. These were the scabs.

5

'I'D RATHER BE A PICKET THAN A SCAB'

'I'd rather be a picket than a scab' was the first line of a tune sung by striking miners while on picket duty. This, along with other songs, helped keep spirits up during what could be the tedium of a long day waiting around. Any violence which erupted outside the collieries was usually due to ongoing attempts by police to escort working miners (scabs) through the gates. Pickets were determined to stop scab coaches from crossing over their line, while police were equally determined to get them through. Coach windows were covered in wire mesh to provide protection from the volley of stones and bricks hurled by pickets as the vehicle inched forward. This scenario would be repeated at the end of the day when the coaches emerged out of the colliery gates.

'Once a scab always a scab' is a saying still used in mining communities to describe those who crossed picket lines during the strike. They were, and still are, reviled by ex-striking miners and their families.

'We were fighting for everybody's jobs, not just our own', explains Bob Collier. 'The strike was on behalf of all miners. It was to keep the pits open for future generations. We knew that if our pits closed there'd be no jobs for our sons, our grandsons.'

Eric Eaton adds:

We just couldn't make them see what was going to happen. They were so gullible. They believed what the government was telling them, which was that the Nottinghamshire pits would not be closed down. We kept warning them that the pits would go. They'd be jobless. They ignored us but later came

54

Police escort a
'scab' coach at
Cortonwood
Colliery
(*courtesy of
Rhoda Allen*).

grovelling when the pits were closed, just as we had said. Not that long after the strike they got a letter from Thatcher thanking them for not striking and also telling them that their pit was about to be shut down. They had laughed in our faces and waved bank notes at us because they knew how much we were struggling to survive. They just hadn't been able to get it into their heads that we were fighting to keep their jobs as well as our own.

The particular thing I'll never understand is how, when they heard about the deaths of Davy Jones and then Joe Green, could they bring themselves to keep working? It was totally disrespectful. They were continuing to support a system which had brought about the deaths of two innocent young lads. They had no principles.

Gradually, as the year moved on, an increasing number of striking miners were creeping back into work. For those who remained strong it was heartbreaking to see. Old friends became enemies and these divisions still remain today. Whole families were torn apart and still remain so. Fathers have refused to speak to their scab sons, as have brothers if one of them had scabbed.

Steven Metcalfe, son of Derbyshire striking miner Ian, was seven in 1984. He remembers the hostility within his community:

Everybody knew who the scabs were. One day I was out playing with a friend. His dad was a scab. Suddenly his dad came up, grabbed him and

Badges were produced for those who stayed out the length of the strike.

shouted, 'I told you NOT to play with strikers' kids!' My friend was in real trouble and was made to stay indoors.

Kay Foster's father was a miner at Frickley Colliery in Yorkshire:

One memory I have isn't very nice. I was about five or six and we were practising for the school Christmas play. Me and my best friend were talking. I said, 'Does your dad work?' and she said, 'Yes', to which I replied, 'Well your dad's a scab then!' – and I wouldn't speak to her for the rest of the day. I went home and told my parents that night who had to explain to me that her dad wasn't a scab because he wasn't a miner, he worked in a pub!'

Sharon James, also the daughter of a Yorkshire miner:

I wouldn't say it was drummed into us that we had to ignore scab kids. It was more that we could see what our parents were going through. My mum used to cry a lot because she was worried sick that we'd lose our house if the mortgage payments fell behind. We'd see the scabs' kids coming into school with new clothes, while my brothers and me had to wear clothes from charity shops. We had to wear worn-out shoes with cardboard stuffed inside to cover the holes. Sometimes the scab kids would start showing-off about their new toys or about how they were going on holiday soon. Our parents couldn't afford any of that sort of thing.

It was the responsibility of the police to ensure that a working miner was able to get into his colliery and this was the case even if he was the only one. Whole convoys of police cars and vans were sometimes deployed to escort just one or two miners. Impractical as this might seem, it was crucial for Margaret Thatcher to send out signals that the government would not give way. Often a police officer would stand guard outside the home of a scab for days at a time. The pickets, however, would wait for their moment. Sooner or later the officer would depart, leaving the pickets free to smash windows and daub slogans over the walls and front door of the house. Scabs' houses soon came to resemble small fortresses, with boarded up windows, mesh-covered doors and barbed-wire fences. After the strike most scabs left the neighbourhood but there were some who stayed behind and who are still ignored by former pickets and their families. In many areas there is a similar situation between striking miners and their families versus police officers and theirs.

Scab house, Yorkshire.

Scab house, Yorkshire (*courtesy of Bruce Wilson*).

There were occasions when working miners would resort to lies and even camouflage to avoid being labelled a scab. Some would leave the house wearing a suit and tie as if dressed for the office, having told neighbours they had a new job in town. Others would buy badges especially made for the striking miners and pin them onto their jackets as if in solidarity with the strike. These deceptions never lasted long, however, as most of the pit villages were tightly bound communities where everybody knew everybody else's business.

In areas where striking miners were in a minority, especially in Leicestershire and Nottinghamshire, pickets found they were on the receiving end of much hostility from the working miners and their families, who viewed them as disruptive trouble-causers.

'The scabs and their wives hated us', says Charlie Cibor and continues:

I remember one particular incident when I'd managed to get into Nottinghamshire with some other flying pickets. We'd been told that a load of scabs were in their local miners' welfare club, so we waited nearby. Sometimes it was still possible to talk to scabs, to reason with them. They would take on board what we were saying and join us. On this occasion though, we didn't get the chance. We'd been spotted by a big group of scab wives and they came over and attacked us. They were really laying into us and all we could do was try to protect ourselves. We couldn't fight back because they were women.

The government had brought in new anti-strike laws when Margaret Thatcher had been preparing for her showdown with the miners but some old and virtually forgotten laws were also dredged up if they were deemed potentially useful. One of these was the Victorian 'besetting' law (more properly known as 'besetting and watching') which is similar to modern-day stalking laws. It was used to prevent striking miners from having any association with working miners, including eye contact. David Ayrton remembers it being used quite widely:

> I myself witnessed a Silverwood miner being arrested under this law. He'd been walking his dogs and stopped outside the home of a scab. Police grabbed him and charged him with 'Besetting the home of a working miner.'

This situation often descended into near farce when striking miners would cut slits into newspaper pages, allowing them to secretly spy on their enemies' movements while pretending to read.

There was one scab in particular who was making a name for himself. Chris Butcher, from Bevercotes Colliery in Nottinghamshire, was being

Anonymous letter sent from a scab to a Kent striking miner (*courtesy of Aylesham Resource Centre*).

Striking miner's wife protesting against Silver Birch (*courtesy of the NUM*).

paid by businessmen to travel round the country attempting to persuade groups of striking miners to return to work. He gained the nickname 'Silver Birch' (thought to be a reference to his prematurely grey hair) although in parts of Yorkshire he was also known as 'Dutch Elm', after the disease which causes trees to rot and die. Even after his pit was closed down he continued to maintain that he never regretted his actions.

In Nottinghamshire there still exists the divide between striking and non-striking miners but for those outside the county it is as if the striking miners never existed and both Leicestershire and Nottinghamshire are referred to as 'Scabland'. At football matches, for example, opponents still chant, 'Scabs! Scabs!' whenever a Nottinghamshire team is playing. Eric Eaton explains the hurt felt by him and his colleagues that the county is still known only for its scabs:

> We constituted nearly a third of the Notts miners and we suffered a lot because we stuck to our principles. All that seems to have been forgotten but I suppose that's the way it is.
> We have a way of telling who scabbed during the strike: when you look at a scab he won't meet your gaze. Instead he'll look down at the ground. Striking miners, however, always walk around with their heads held high.

Perhaps Darren Moore, of the Leicestershire 'Dirty Thirty', should have the last word:

> The scabs hated us. I think they knew they were morally wrong which made them hate us all the more. I like to think that I was their conscience.

6

THE WOMEN

'Rosie the Riveter' is the now iconic image (originally titled 'We Can Do It') produced by J. Howard Miller in 1944 to inspire a generation of American women to become involved in the war effort. Throughout history it has been the case that during times of national crisis, women have emerged as a strong force and so it proved again during the miners' strike. Women played a direct role both on and off the picket lines. Several have described how

'Rosie the Riveter'.

Cortonwood Women Against Pit Closures (*courtesy of Rhoda Allen*).

they felt as if they had been 'sleep-walking' through their lives up until the strike, never questioning their roles as mothers and homemakers.

Joyce Sheppard, of the Yorkshire branch of Women Against Pit Closures (WAPC), describes the mood leading up to the strike:

> There was a sense of foreboding all around. The steelworks nearby had already gone and there was a real threat of unemployment. We were very worried about our futures. We had children to think about. We had mortgages. As well as the fear there was anger; anger that our livelihoods were about to be taken away. We were just ordinary, working-class women who felt that our families, our children, were under attack. It was our job to fight back and defend them.

Women's groups formed very quickly, without the need for committees or formal meetings. The women managed to avoid administrative bureaucracy and, as Joyce says, '… just rolled up our sleeves and got on with it'. Very soon a network of support groups had been established throughout the country. Kay Sutcliffe, a Kent miner's wife, describes how she was able to quickly summon up help:

> I'd organised a group of supporters during the 1974 strike. We called ourselves the Aylesham Ladies' – yes, 'Ladies' (laughs) – Action Group. As soon as the 1984 strike began I contacted the women to see if they'd like to get involved again. I arranged a meeting and expected around ten of them to turn up. In fact fifty women arrived. It was wonderful.
>
> We decided we'd head for Nottingham but the people at the NUM instructed us to go to Leicestershire. Two busloads of us went up there, including some women from other pits, and we were accompanied by a BBC TV crew. We arrived in Coalville and, although some were cheering, there was a lot of booing and a lot were against us. We weren't allowed in the local meeting hall, so we had to have our meeting in a car park. The Leicestershire miners' wives were jeering and shouting at us to clear off – remember, there were only thirty men out on strike there. In the end we did manage to get our point across to a few of them that their men's jobs would soon be on the line. Some of them were listening and they began to understand what we were trying to do.

Soup kitchens were set up and quickly became the heart of the community. Everybody congregated here, not only to eat but also to share and gather

Soup kitchen (*courtesy of Peter Arkell*).

information. Because the soup kitchen played such a central role, the women who worked there were often the first to hear news of what was happening and were able to spread the word – a hugely important task during a pre-mobile phone and pre-Internet society.

There was often a strict hierarchy within these kitchens. Many younger, less experienced women would find themselves being reprimanded for carelessness or for being too slow. This was a matriarchal community where younger women might have to earn their stripes and prove that they were worthwhile. When preparing as many as 400 meals a day, every day, speed and efficiency were essential.

The kitchen at Worsbrough, near Barnsley, opened on 28 June. It received some funding from the NUM but also relied on donations from street collections made in nearby towns and cities. On average this kitchen served 280 meals every day, the weekly cost being around £700.

Typical Menu for the Worsbrough Soup Kitchen:

Pie, chips and peas
Fruit flan
Tea, bread

Liver and onions with chips
Rice pudding
Tea, bread

Fish, chips and peas
Fruit pie and custard
Tea, bread

(Reproduced with permission of Barnsley Archives & Local Studies)

The kitchen would also provide packed lunches for those on picket-line duty. One Yorkshire picket recalls how, on hot August days, the pickets would look forward to returning to their local kitchen where there would be a vat (in the form of a tin bath) of freshly-squeezed orange juice, complete with the remains of the oranges floating on the surface.

After a seven-hour shift on the picket line this was heaven. We were that hot and thirsty. Then in winter we'd come back freezing cold and there would be this vat of hot soup. Just what we needed.

These kitchens played an essential role but many women began to realise that they could become active in other areas. For one thing they had to raise funds and collect money to buy supplies. One woman recalls:

> It were a constant battle, a real headache, trying to decide what were today's priorities. So should we buy milk or should we buy some mince? I don't think people on the outside realised just how tough it was. I don't think they believed that often we just didn't have enough food and that sometimes our kids would go to bed hungry. Don't forget our benefits had been stopped. People just wouldn't believe this were happening. It were more like Victorian days.

It has often been said that the strike politicised women but Anne Scargill, of Yorkshire WAPC and Barnsley Miners' Wives, rejects this idea, maintaining that women were already politicised by virtue of their being working class. They were from generations'-old socialist families and the miners' strike provided the chance for them to get involved in a more direct way.

Women began to join the picket lines or else form their own. They also began to venture out further afield, realising that, to begin with at least, the police largely ignored them as it seemed they posed no threat. As Joyce Sheppard recounts:

> It was much easier for we women to cross the borders which had been set up between one county and another. We were below the police radar and we

Eppleton Women Against Pit Closures (*courtesy of Florence Anderson*).

Miners were far more likely to stay out on strike if they were supported by their wives. Gaye Wilson, mother of a toddler and baby, was determined to back up her husband, Bruce, who stayed out until the end.

took advantage of that. So, for example, we were able to cross from Yorkshire into Nottinghamshire and back again with little difficulty. It was essential that we could contact others in different areas. It was important to show solidarity with other strikers and their families. We didn't have mobile phones or Internet. The situation changed from day to day and help was needed on picket lines all over the country.

We learned all sorts of tricks to outwit the powers that be. The women from Greenham Common came to support us and taught us a lot. I have nothing but respect for them. To working-class miners' wives, the Greenham Common women seemed like exotic creatures. They taught us to be well organised in our dealings with the police, even down to always having the name and phone number of a solicitor on you when you went out demonstrating in case of arrest. They knew how to handle themselves in the face of police harassment and intimidation. They were comrades fighting the same enemy and it was good to know we had support from other groups.

Women from various unions became active in fundraising whether or not they were part of the mining community. Sometimes it was just one individual who stepped forward to drive the cause forward. Simone Moore was working for the Inland Revenue in Leicester when the strike began:

I had no contacts in the mining world, I wasn't a miner's wife (although I would become one some time later!) and knew no one. I was shop steward for my union and, after seeing and hearing what was happening to the miners, I knew I had to take a stand. I knew I must try to persuade everybody I knew to become involved. I obviously couldn't join a miners' wives group and I lived in the city, which made it a bit difficult to maintain contact with the collieries out in Leicestershire. Sometimes I felt like a bit of a lone voice but this was a hugely important issue.

I'd come from a working-class background and I knew never to cross a picket line. When I was a teenager I gave my school dinner-money to some striking firemen. That was my first experience of showing solidarity. I just felt compelled to do it ... I don't know why. Some of my school-friends would roll their eyes a bit (laughs).

Many women, such as Tyne and Wear councillor Florence Anderson, were prepared to be arrested repeatedly in order to support the strike. Florence, a miner's wife and chair of the Eppleton Miners' Wives Support Group, was arrested at Eppleton pit after throwing eggs at a van carrying a scab into work. She was found guilty of using 'threatening behaviour' for which she was conditionally discharged for a year and ordered to pay costs. After being sentenced she announced that she would be heading straight back to the picket line.

Once it had been recognised that the women were a force to be reckoned with, any tolerance the police had shown swiftly came to an end. The women soon discovered that they would be treated the same as the men.

Joyce recounts:

The police didn't treat us with more leniency just because we were women. On the contrary. Many women were arrested, strip searched and given the third-degree. They'd be put in prison cells where the toilets had no doors so that everyone could see what you were doing. It was humiliating.

Other women tell of the verbal abuse meted out to them:

The police would shout things at us. We'd be walking our kids to school and the police would shout horrible things and jeer at us. I hated my kids hearing it. Sometimes they waved money at us, or threw coins, laughing because they knew we were so hard-up.

Flyers asking for support were produced by the Royston Miners' Wives Group (*reproduced with permission of Barnsley Archives & Local Studies*).

> MINERS' WIVES OPPOSED TO PIT CLOSURES
> ROYSTON DRIFT BRANCH
>
> ROYSTON MINERS' WIVES GROUP CALL UPON ROYSTON TRADERS AND BUSINESS PEOPLE TO MAKE CONTRIBUTIONS OF PRODUCE OR CASH WHICH WILL BE USED TO HELP FAMILIES AFFECTED BY THE STRIKE THROUGH THIS DIFFICULT PERIOD.
>
> DONATIONS SHOULD BE MADE TO MEMBERS OF THE WIVES GROUP OR TO ROYSTON SOCIAL WORKINGMEN'S CLUB (THE BUSH) GODLEY STREET.
>
> SUPPORTED BY ROYSTON'S LABOUR COUNCILLORS AND BY ROYSTON AND CARLTON LABOUR PARTY.
>
> THANK YOU!

The miners' strike quite literally opened up women's horizons. Those who had never or rarely left their area suddenly found that they were travelling to regions unknown. They were going to other towns and cities, including London, in order to raise funds. Joyce talks of the time she was in York:

> I'd been standing with the other women, shaking my collecting tin at passers-by. A policeman came up and moved us on. He told us we were upsetting the tourists. 'Tourists?' I thought. Then I realised, we were right next to York Minster. 'Well,' I thought to myself, 'I've always wanted to come to York and I might never get the chance to come again.' I thought, 'Right then, I'm going to take myself off and look round York Minster!' – and that's what I did. Went in and looked round, carrying my collection tin. I nearly missed the bus back!

Another striking miner's wife, Jean Phillips from Armthorpe, Yorkshire, recalls being both nervous and excited about going down to attend a London rally:

> We knew we were there for a purpose but it was also like having a big day out. When we got to London we were amazed at the amount of people who had turned up. It was wonderful to feel that we weren't on our own in our village: there were thousands of others just like us.

Mothers often felt guilty about breaking away from their maternal roles. They were concerned that the children were being neglected, especially if both parents were travelling away to take action on picket lines. On the other hand, unless the men's jobs were saved, the outlook for their families was bleak. The women felt compelled to fight for their menfolk's jobs for the sake of the children. Besides, it was usually the case that there would be a friend or neighbour somewhere on hand to look after the children while the parents were away. The neighbourhood had evolved into a large and caring community.

Jean Phillips at a London rally (*courtesy of Leslie Phillips*).

The Eppleton Women's Strike Committee 1984 (*courtesy of Florence Anderson, front row, fourth from the left*).

Clipstone Pit (Nottingshire) Women's Support Group (*courtesy of Doug Broadfoot*).

Most women's support groups made a banner such as this one created by the Royston Drift women (*reproduced with permission of Barnsley Archives & Local Studies*).

If community bonds were being formed, however, marriages were often being torn apart. The stress of worrying about money and fear of the future sometimes became too much. There was the constant threat of unemployment and many men were anxiously waiting for their cases to come up in court if they had been arrested. One picket from the Yorkshire village of Goldthorpe had been arrested and spent two days in jail:

> Then I was told that my case would come up at some point but nobody knew when. I spent ten months of hell waiting to see what were going to happen to me. I'd been arrested at Orgreave. It were like it was hanging over me all the time. I was worried sick I'd end up in prison. Didn't know how my wife and two kids would manage. I didn't go to prison but in the end I had a breakdown and my wife left anyway.

Other women left because they were angry with their striking husband or partner, holding him responsible for the financial hardship caused. Striking Nottinghamshire miner, Bob Collier, explains:

Kay Sutcliffe of Women Against Pit Closures, Snowdown Colliery, Kent (2014). Kay retired from her work as a community development officer for Dover District Council in 2011. She now works as a volunteer to support a local charity, is a parish councillor and is treasurer of a community forum in Aylesham.

The women could make all the difference as to whether a man went on strike or stayed out on strike. 'Petticoat power' it was called, and it was a powerful thing. Some women couldn't understand why they and their kids should have to suffer and felt the man's first priority should be his family. They weren't able to see that he was fighting to keep his job so that he could support his wife and children. It caused a lot of stress in a relationship. If the woman was supportive of the strike then there was a good chance that the miner would stay out and see it through 'til the bitter end.

Many women became the breadwinner, either increasing their hours if they were already working or taking on new jobs. This sometimes became a source of resentment for men who were already questioning their own position as providers within their family. Many men saw a new side to their wives and girlfriends and found themselves reappraising the relationship. Sometimes there would be confrontation when the strike ended because women were often unwilling to revert to their former selves and refused to take on their former roles. Most men, however, were proud of and grateful to their wives and partners. A deeper bond was formed which made the relationship stronger but it is perhaps inevitable that, in many cases, there would be casualties.

7

AGGIE CURRY

My husband was a miner at Armthorpe pit when the strike began. I'd never been that political and just used to vote Labour because that's what you did in the mining background I came from. When the strike started I thought it would just be like the other short-lived, local strikes which happened from time to time and I wasn't interested. I thought it was just the 'red raggers', which is what we used to call the militant ones, kicking off again. Then I met a woman who was fund-raising for the striking miners and she persuaded me to go to a meeting. Seeing the determination on the faces of the lasses there got me hooked and I knew I had to get involved. From then on I was totally committed to the strike and it made me angry that the rest of the unions wouldn't come out to support us even though the miners had always done it for others.

I helped out at the soup kitchen and joined picket lines all over the place. Some of the miners warned me not to get too aggressive with the police or I'd be arrested. Well, I didn't want to hold back, so I didn't and I shouted what I liked. It got physical as well and I was pushing and shoving on the picket lines along with the men. The police had me marked as a trouble causer, and once when I wanted to leave the line to go and buy a packet of fags, a cop insisted on coming with me so he could keep an eye on me. On the way to the shop a scab's wife spat in my face.

Yes, the poverty was bad but I'm a survivor. We lost our house, went without food and other basic necessities that normally you take for granted. As far as I'm concerned Thatcher took food out of my kids' mouths. She thought if she made life hard for families then the women would persuade the men to go back to work. Well she was wrong. I used to go fundraising everywhere including London, where, on the whole, we received fantastic support. One day I passed a building which had a sign saying National Union of Journalists,

Aggie Curry, wife of a Yorkshire striking miner, joined picket lines and became an activist.

so in I went. Wherever I went I'd go to union offices, trying to build up support from them for the miners, and when I found I was outside the NUJ offices, I went straight in to ask for help and they gave it. We were so poor and that winter we were very cold but we weren't going to give in. It was just as difficult for a long time after the strike because we then had to start paying arrears and sorting our debts out.

The community pulled together and we all helped one another. When my dad died the soup kitchen provided the snap [food] for the gathering after the funeral. I tell you what: people say Thatcher destroyed communities – well she didn't destroy MY f–ing community! The longer the strike went on the more determined we were to stay out. People were asking me to give talks about the strike, and I was even asked to speak in Denmark. The first time I was terrified. It was at Sheffield University and my legs were shaking. I had to stand on a box. My stomach was churning and I had to keep clearing my throat. I can't remember what I said but I do remember that at the end I got a standing ovation. My dad had just died but my mum was in the audience and we looked at one another for a long time while they were clapping. A scab's wife had also been asked to come and speak that day but I said, 'What I've got to say comes from the heart – not from a piece of paper like hers.'

The strike made me political and I went to Greenham Common with Anne Scargill and Betty Cook. I organised a mass demo and rally during the strike in my village and was convinced nobody would turn up. I needn't have worried though because on the day it was so packed with people you could barely move. The strike affected me and my family for many years because we'd lost our house and it took us a long time to get another and pay off debts we'd built up when we had no income coming in. I've a big collection of badges and I was offered £1,000 for them but I'd never sell because the pits and the strike are part of me now.

8

BETTY COOK AND ANNE SCARGILL

A nne Scargill and Betty Cook were prominent activists during the miners' strike and were part of Barnsley Miners' Wives and WAPC. Both women continue to campaign for social justice and civil liberties issues.

BETTY COOK

I'd been a shop steward for my union but it was my activities during the strike which really gave me the confidence to go out into the wider world and campaign for social justice. I took a community studies course at a local college, followed by my studying Social Policy and Sociology at the

Betty Cook.

University of Sheffield. It had always been my parents' dream that I would go to university but I never believed I would. It was the strike which changed the direction of my life in so many ways. My experiences in the strike led me on to champion students' right at my university and to encourage the younger ones to take on more of a role. I went out to work in a Romanian orphanage and then, once back in England, I continued with the fight to defend our collieries. My mother was quite dependent on me at this stage but I managed to combine caring for her with my campaigning. During 1992–3 a group of us occupied Parkside Colliery in Lancashire where I tended to be the one dealing with phone calls from the press and media. I joined Anne Scargill, Aggie Curry and others in setting up a camp outside the Department of Trade and Industry in London. We got a brazier going on the pavement outside Michael Heseltine's office and the police were running round in circles trying to deal with us!

When the remaining collieries were privatised I was interviewed by the BBC, and I warned that privatisation would mean that health and safety standards would drop. I predicted that there would be more accidents and deaths and I was proved to be right. There were three fatalities within the next three years. I could never have dreamt that the first of these would be my own son, Donny, who was killed in a roof fall in 2008 at Kellingley. This was followed by the death of a lad named Ian who was killed when some machinery fell on him and, later, another named Gerry was buried under coal. UK Coal would deny any culpability but I maintain that there should have been ongoing refresher training courses. Sometimes men were put back into an area of work which they hadn't done for many years and, to me, it seems obvious that they needed re-training first. The death of my son lead to me being pursued by the media and the pressure almost completely overwhelmed me.

As part of the Barnsley Miners' Wives group, Anne and I travelled to the USA to meet the women of the United Mineworkers of America. Through them we learned about Mary 'Mother' Jones, an Irish-American community worker who, in 1902, was labelled the 'most dangerous woman in America' due to her work in organising protests by mine workers against the mine owners. The organisation is still very active and the women are known as the Daughters of Mother Jones. Anne and I wanted to follow their example and so we now also use this title as well as Barnsley Miners' Wives. Our group have adopted a hospital in Cuba and we're involved in fundraising for this. I'm now employed in working in educational support and I also work as a volunteer with the Salvation Army. I shall continue to campaign for workers' and civil rights, partly in memory of my son and also because it's a fight which is becoming increasingly important all over the world.

ANNE

My dad had always taught me that you should never, ever cross a picket line and I learned that lesson well. Early on in the strike I joined the picket line at Silverhill pit in Nottinghamshire where I'd somehow managed to cross the border from Yorkshire. Later I would join different picket lines and I occupied the offices at the Armthorpe pit. I was arrested several times throughout the strike and the first time I was strip-searched, so they could look for weapons, had a strong effect on me. It made me into a bad 'un. What I mean by that is I felt that if I was going to be humiliated and treated like scum then I'd no longer hold back or show any respect for them. On that particular day nothing much seemed to be happening on the picket line but then the police started putting on their chinstraps as if they were getting ready for something. A lot more police arrived and started making arrests. I asked why, so they arrested me as well but I refused to give my name until they formally charged me with something. At the police station we were

Anne Scargill.

78

held in a dog compound before the strip-searches began. I was even asked which newspapers I read. These sort of experiences made us tougher and more determined. Later we'd join picket lines elsewhere with no hesitation. When the print workers came out at Wapping in 1986 we just said, 'Let's go!' … and we did. Looking back, all these years later, I sometimes think, 'Was that really me doing those things?'

One of the funniest days at that time was when a group of us went to protest outside Michael Heseltine's office at the DTI. We set up a camp and got a brazier going. A big white van from Yorkshire TV arrived and then a policeman appeared. Well … the look on that bobby's face … he was speechless! We'd just made tea, so I offered him a cup. The result was that he contacted his mates and a load more bobbies arrived. They immediately contacted the fire brigade because of our brazier. We pleaded with the firemen, 'Oh don't go and put our fire out, we'll be so cold!', so they left! By now the windows of the building were turning black because of all the nasty smoke from the cheap, foreign coal we were using. The police inspector arrives, furious. We gave him some leaflets to read but he throws them on the brazier. He didn't want a cup of tea either. We could see he was going to arrest us, so I and another member of our group, Brenda Nixon, chained ourselves to the front door of the building. As a matter of fact we hadn't done it properly and the lock didn't work. The inspector could easily have undone it but he didn't look. Instead he calls the fire brigade to come and cut the chains, so back they come. Same lads as before. Nope, they refused to help because they wouldn't cross our picket line. They sat in their fire engine and watched while the bobbies used the cutters on our chains. No success – the cutters were blunt! Another pair was sent for and by now the inspector was nearly beside himself.

They finally managed to arrest us and, as we were led off, we saw huge amounts of black smoke covering the building as the police used fire extinguishers on the brazier. We were sat on a form in a row, like school children, at the police station and charged with criminal damage. The bobbies had to empty a great big bag of stuff we'd brought with us and make a list of all the contents. There were all sorts of things in there, including somebody's spare underwear and nineteen-odd earrings. We were trying not to laugh too much as the bobby wrote it all down: it took him three-quarters of an hour. Good times.

9

SURVIVAL AND SOLIDARITY

One day we were told a load of gays were coming to join us on the picket line. Well, we were a bunch of rough, tough Yorkshire lads. We'd never had owt to do with gays. I think there was one who worked at our pit but that was all. We couldn't understand why they were coming. Anyway, their coach arrived and out jumped all these well-built, muscular blokes. We hadn't been expecting that!

We decided to have a bit of fun so we started shouting things to them to take the mickey. We were having a laugh about them being gay but then a group of them came across and stood with us. They told us they were here to show solidarity with us because they were an oppressed minority just like we now were. They said they knew that Thatcher was targeting the miners and that we should all be standing together to fight for our rights. Well, after that, we had nothing but respect for them.

Charlie Cibor, Markham Main Colliery, Yorkshire

The strike changed miners' attitudes towards women and towards other sections of society. Old prejudices were broken down as various minority groups declared their support for the striking miners. The Asian community, for instance, followed the gay community's example by joining picket lines and providing financial help. Although other unions had been reluctant to take industrial action on behalf of the miners, there were several, such as the NUJ, which contributed financially. All this provided a big morale boost for the striking miners and their families because they now knew they were not alone in their fight. They felt part of a wider society.

NUM leaflet sent to striking miners, encouraging them to stay out on strike and telling them to ignore 'bribe' letters issued by the Coal Board (*reproduced with kind permission of Barnsley Archives & Local Studies*).

Darren Moore:

When the strike began we started trying to work out where we could get help. Three of us went to Leicester County Hall where there was a NALGO meeting. From there we discovered that there was a Leicester support group who helped us throughout the strike. Other Leicester unions helped as well and Leicester City Council gave us a room to use.

After a while we found that, because there were so few of us, sometimes we had more than we needed and so we'd share it. We chose to be 'twinned' with two Yorkshire pits, Goldthorpe and Hickleton Main. We took money and presents up there at Christmas.

Spreading the word was a big part of fundraising and, because he was young and single with no family to support, it was Darren who tended to travel around giving talks and asking for help. On one occasion he spoke at a thousand-strong conference meeting where, despite feeling nervous, he was loudly applauded. As with many striking miners, he was discovering skills he never knew he had.

The poverty was real. There was worry about not being able to afford basic essentials, including food, along with the constant anxiety that the house might be repossessed. As the months dragged on, however, it became evident that there was a great deal of sympathy in the wider community for the striking miners and their families. Shops and businesses, aware that the strike would not last forever, were careful not to upset what were, essentially, their customers and made special allowances. Local shops donated food for soup kitchens, and companies allowed their employees to take time out to go on marches and attend rallies. Pubs up and down the country provided cheap beer, and building societies put mortgages on hold. Support was particularly strong in areas such as Yorkshire where almost everyone had a relation or friend in the mining industry. Local councils often provided financial support in one way or another. Some issued vouchers to pay for school uniforms and others brought in reduced bus fares for the families of striking miners. In Armthorpe, Yorkshire, the council indicated which trees in nearby woods could be felled for firewood by marking them with a white cross. Not all businesses were supportive, however. Many miners did lose their houses and there was the constant fear of the bailiff.

Some MPs joined lawyers who were working ex gratia to aid striking miners. Tony Benn, MP for Chesterfield, intervened when some of his constituents were arrested on the picket lines; Bolsover MP Dennis Skinner managed to stop the repossession of a house by the local council. Celebrities of the day also became involved, and when the plight of the striking miners became international news, US rock legend Bruce Springsteen, amongst others, donated money. In many ways it was a heady time for the men and their families who were struggling even to afford food.

The NUM sometimes helped with transport costs (*reproduced with permission of Barnsley Archives & Local Studies*).

Italian leaflet supporting the strike (*courtesy of Darren Moore*).

Manifestazioni di solidarietà con i minatori inglesi

Da ormai un anno i minatori britannici sono in sciopero per respingere il piano della Thatcher che vuole la chiusura di 70 pozzi e la liquidazione di più di 70 mila posti di lavoro.

Per schiacciare questa prodigiosa lotta, padronato e governo inglesi, stanno usando ogni mezzo a loro disposizione: migliaia gli arresti e le denunce, centinaia i feriti dalle cariche della polizia.

I MINATORI POSSONO ANCORA FARCELA!

Many miners diversified, finding that their skills in other areas could be used to make money. Some painted and sold pictures and others carved walking sticks from wood they found lying around near the colliery. Some sculpted and sold ornaments made from coal. Kay Foster's mother and grandmother set up a small business making and selling cheap tracksuits, which sold well. People grew their own vegetables, either giving away, swapping or selling any surplus.

Previously argumentative neighbours now pulled together to share resources. Sympathetic farmers would allow striking miners to pull up vegetables in their fields. There were some who developed poaching skills in order to live off the land. A Yorkshire miner's wife remembers:

> One winter's night my husband's friend (they were both striking miners) appeared at the back door, saying he'd got some food for us. He comes in and places a dead sheep on the kitchen table. A whole sheep! With its wool on and everything! I told him, 'No thank you very much, I don't want it! Take it away!' He was a bit offended, I think, but there was no way I was going to start cutting up a whole sheep!

Pig carved out of coal (*courtesy of Richard Ormrod*).

UK striking miners' wives were the guests of miners' wives in East Germany (*courtesy of Jenny Metcalfe*).

Another Yorkshire miner recalls, 'I was always out catching rabbits and pheasants. Sometimes I got a deer and we had venison. My kids were living off these and now they can't stand the taste of any of them!'

International aid and offers of help began to pour in. Great convoys of supplies arrived from different countries and trips abroad were arranged for the miners, their wives and their children. What was then East Germany and the USSR were particularly helpful. 'The Soviets were the ones who sent loads of food parcels,' remembers Kay Sutcliffe, a Kent miner's wife, 'while the French always seemed to send a lot of toys, especially at Christmas. It would mostly be dolls and footballs.'

Charlie Cibor remembers:

There was one time when a massive lorry arrived in our neighbourhood. It was parked there for two weeks. I can't remember where from exactly but it was somewhere abroad. Inside there were hundreds of pairs of shoes and everyone was told to take some.

There were two types of donated tinned foods in particular which, it seems, were repeatedly used to the point of overkill: Irish stew was one, the other being mince with onions.

'We got so sick of it', explains Steven Metcalfe. 'My mum kept telling us that it was useful because it was versatile but my dad and me got to the point where we really couldn't stand it. I think lots of other families felt the same. It seemed to be everywhere', he laughs.

Striking miners, their families and other supporters took part in street collections and rallies. There were large mass gatherings in London where coalfields from all over the country were represented.

Ian Metcalfe recalls, 'There were a few people who shouted at us to clear off or get back to work but, on the whole, people in London gave us fantastic support and were very generous.'

These London rallies were a way of uniting the collieries and building solidarity amongst the striking miners. Charlie Cibor recalls:

> The pit bands came as well. Sometimes, on special occasions back home, there'd be different bands playing but they had to be kept apart because they'd all be playing different music. On this day in London, though, all the bands joined together and played the same tunes. It really was one of the most moving things I've ever heard or seen and a lot of other people said the same.

Phil Auckland of Houghton Main colliery in Yorkshire remembers a particular incident in London:

> We had these big buckets for passers-by to throw money into. This woman came up, very dishevelled and scruffy looking. She took a sandwich out of her bag, placed it in the bucket then walked off. I bent down, took the sandwich and found it was stuffed with £20 notes. She'd made a sandwich using money! I looked for her but she'd gone. Disappeared into the crowd.

Cyril Brazier of Snowdown Colliery, Kent:

> Two or three of us were collecting outside a supermarket. We were asking shoppers to buy a tin of food for the miners and put it in this big bin we had. Anyway, this old lady comes up and asks what we're doing. I explained and she opened her purse, took out 10p and chucked it in the bin. She then

NATIONAL UNION OF JOURNALISTS Brian Kay
Branch Treasurer
93 Mexborough Place
Leeds
LS7 3EB
Tel: 629243

Leeds Branch

November 26, 1984.

Dear Aggie,
At a meeting earlier this month, Leeds branch
of the NUJ resolved to 'adopt' the Armthorpe support
group.

I am therefore delighted to enclose an
initial donation of £65 towards the support of your
group. The cheque has been left open, partially because
no-one seemed able to tell me who to make it payable
to, but also because you might also appreciate some
flexibility in this. I would, however, be grateful
if you could acknowledge its receipt, as well as giving
some indication as to how further donations should be
made out.

I sincerely hope the branch finds itself in
a position to make another contribution before Christmas.
Best wishes to you all.
Yours,

Brian M. kay

Donation letters to the Armthorpe striking miners.

NEWS GROUP NEWSPAPERS LTD.
(NEWS OF THE WORLD) ELECTRICAL CHAPEL (SUN)
E.E.T.P.U.

Phone : 01-353 3030

30 Bouverie St.
London, EC4Y 8DE

Dear Friends & Comarades
Enclosed find cheque for £100 as a donation
towards your welfare fund

We trust this contribution will assist in
some way to making things a bit easier, even as the
strike is over the hardship must remain for some time.

We wish you the greatest of luck and our
admiration

Yours Fraternally

C. H

helped herself to a couple of tins of food and walked off. We were laughing so much that we hadn't got the heart to call her back.

It had been a long, hot summer in 1984 but as autumn and winter approached, striking miners and their families had to face the misery of no heating. They had been used to receiving a coal allowance or help with fuel costs as part of their wages but the government had ensured that this would be cancelled. Furthermore, striking miners themselves were no longer entitled to social security payments. Instead Margaret Thatcher instructed the NUM to provide financial support, possibly in the knowledge that to do so would bankrupt the union. No money was forthcoming from the NUM and the miners were simply unable to afford heating. Families faced the approaching winter with dread. This had become a war of attrition.

Coal-picking, also known as 'coal-riddling', became a regular chore for families, including children. This involved scavenging for bits of coal on pit waste tips and was a dangerous task, sometimes resulting in injury and death. In the Yorkshire village of Goldthorpe, for example, 15-year-old Paul Holmes and his 14-year-old brother, Darren, were killed when they were buried under a heap of dirt and rubble.

Ian Wroe explains:

It wasn't just the striking miners who went coal-picking, everybody went. There was just no coal at all, anywhere. Either the pits were closed or they were working with reduced staff. I wasn't a miner, I'd been a steelworker but

Coal-picking in Yorkshire (*courtesy of Rhoda Allen*).

Children coal-picking (*courtesy of Peter Arkell*).

I still needed coal, just like anybody else. I used to head for the big mounds of dirt left each day near a building site. You used to be able to find low-grade bits of coal if you searched through.

As often happens, though, some greedy people ruined it for everybody else. The security guards at the site used to turn a blind eye while a few of us were riddling but then one night somebody turned up with a bloody great van and took loads. The guards weren't so helpful after that.

Anything which could be sold usually was and, when the weather turned cold, anything which could be burned usually was also. These included garden fences and interior house doors. Armthorpe miner's wife Jean Phillips came up with a novel idea purely by accident:

I'd made a stew but the dumplings went wrong. I thought I might as well throw them on the fire, which I did. Well, they burned for ages! I think it must've been the fat in them. So I used that method every now and then. Looking back it's very funny.

Silverwood (Yorkshire) miner's wife, Gaye Wilson, kept a stack of old shoes and clothes by the fireplace ready to burn. 'They burned quite well but the trouble was that they'd sometimes get so hot that the metal grating in the fireplace would melt. You got to know what you could and couldn't burn.'

With the knowledge that there was no money available for children's presents, parents were not looking forward to Christmas. The National Coal Board took advantage of this and tried to tempt striking miners back

EARN IT OR LOSE IT

If you come back to work on or before the 10th of December, and work up to Christmas you could earn, as a face worker over £500 or as a surface worker £395 (see table). And you must work the whole of the last week before Christmas to qualify for Holiday Pay and Service Bonus or you will lose this money forever.

Come back now, you've lost enough already.

Contact your Colliery Manager for shift times and transport arrangements.

GRADE:-	U.1	U.C.1	U.7	S.6
	£	£	£	£
WAGES (incl. BATHING & CHANGING)	265.30	245.50	212.35	192.90
HOLIDAY PAY*	182.42	168.56	147.00	131.74
MAXIMUM BONUS (BASED ON SERVICE)	70.00	70.00	70.00	70.00
TOTAL:-	517.72	484.06	429.35	394.64

*At Cadeby, Silverwood/Steetley and Silverwood where Christmas holiday arrangements are different, holiday pay will be 1/52nd of these figures.

An **NCB** South Yorkshire Area Announcement

BEAT THE TAX MAN COME BACK NOW!

By returning to work on or before 25 February you will have the chance to earn, by the end of the tax year, more than £1000 if you are a faceworker, and over £850 if you work on the surface. This money includes holiday pay earned after four complete weeks back at work. And if you come back anyday of week commencing 25 February – it will be tax free.

After that, your holiday pay will be subject to the tax man's usual percentage.

So beat the tax man and come back NOW.

You won't be alone. More and more men are returning to work every day.

In Yorkshire, over 7000 mineworkers have already given up the strike and across Britain's Coalfields that figure is now 84,000 and still rising.

For shift times and transport arrangements at YOUR UNIT ring the manager – or talk it over with one of the growing army of return-to-work miners.

An **NCB** Announcement.

Leaflets trying to persuade striking miners to return to work (*reproduced with permission of Barnsley Archives & Local Studies*).

Christmas card and donation from the Fire Brigades Union (*reproduced with permission of Barnsley Archives & Local Studies*).

to work by offering a large Christmas bonus. Parents, however, need not have worried: most children (now adults) say that this was one of the best Christmases they ever had. Presents arrived from well-wishers all around the world and mining communities were overwhelmed with gifts of toys and food. Christmas dinners were served in community centres, concerts were organised and neighbours pulled together, determined to make this a good Christmas for the children.

By now, though, an increasing number of miners were returning to work, leaving those still on strike with a feeling of dread. While most children had enjoyed Christmas, their parents had been grimly clinging on to faint hopes

Christmas card from Arthur Scargill (*courtesy of Aylesham Resource Centre*).

N.U.M. H.Q.

To all you good striking miners

As the democratically-elected leader of this Union, I've been given a clear mandate by the vast majority of my members to wish you a very Merry Christmas.

Arthur

Signed on his behalf by:-

Aylesham Womens. Support Group.

Happy Xmas, Best Wishes for the New Year

&

VICTORY TO THE MINERS !!

Christmas Greet

from Arthur Sca & the N.U.M.

in the knowledge that the government were winning. There had been a time, back in October, when it seemed possible that the striking miners might be victorious but members of the pit deputies union, NACODS, had backtracked at the eleventh hour on their decision to take strike action. Lack of support from other unions meant that the miners were increasingly becoming stranded and left out on a limb. The TUC distanced itself from the strike and Labour leader Neil Kinnock earned for himself the nickname 'Kneel' Kinnock for his apparent subservience to the government.

Some striking miners, no longer able to cope, had breakdowns. There were suicides. Many were plunged into despair as their wives deserted them,

Flyers handed out to the public when striking miners went to various towns and cities to collect donations.

SUPPORT THE MINERS
seasons greetings from the
Bolsover
——— *STRIKING MINERS* ———

ARMTHORPE BRANCH NUM
MARKHAM MAIN COLLIERY 1984 STRIKE

Dear Friends,

On behalf of our families and ourselves, we wish you, your families, and friends a very merry Christmas and a happy and peaceful New Year. And on behalf of the National Executive of the National Union of Miners, our 140,000 striking brothers, their wives and their children, we take this opportunity to thank you for the generous support you have given during our ten months of bitter struggle.

Darren Moore, of the 'Dirty Thirty', took on some volunteer work in the probation service after his colliery was closed. He now works as a professional in welfare rights. Of the 'Dirty Thirty' he remarks, 'We're a dwindling bunch but we try to keep in touch. There's always a bond between us even though we might not get to see one another very often.'

Darren and Simone met and married after the strike. Simone has continued to work in community development in areas of deprivation, including old pit villages. She also works in areas of women's aid and domestic violence.

Markham (Derbyshire) picket Ian Metcalfe was arrested several times during the strike. After his pit was closed down he worked in the NHS as a hospital theatre technician. Moving from a coal mine to a clean, sterilised environment, he jokes that he has gone from one extreme to the other.

Ian's wife, Jenny, who was active in the Derbyshire Miners' Wives' group, used to get up at 4.30 a.m. to join the picket line at her local pit before returning home for the school-run. She would then spend the day organising food parcels. After the strike she studied psychology and sociology at a local college and has had several poems published.

taking the children. For others, however, it was the generosity and solidarity shown by many different communities or even random strangers which largely came to define the strike. There is no doubt that striking miners and their families had to endure much hardship and poverty yet it is the kindness, community spirit and compassion shown by others which is more often remembered.

To quote Charles Dickens, 'It was the worst of times, it was the best of times.'

10

NORMAN STRIKE

My family moved from Norfolk to Durham in 1871 to become miners but my grandad threatened that if ever I went down the pits, he'd break my legs. He didn't want me to do this dangerous, difficult work and, to be honest, neither did I. Leaving school at 15, I joined the army but hated it so much that my dad paid £80 to buy me out.

In 1968, despite my grandad's threat, I became a mining apprentice at West Westoe, where my first job was working as a 'tippler' lad. This involved hooking and unhooking tubs full of coal to tip out. I was promoted to 'button' lad, which meant that I was responsible for pressing the button if the conveyor belt, on its way to the shute, ever got stuck. I was very bored and so I took books to read. One day I was so engrossed in what I was reading that I failed to notice the huge blockage caused when the belt snapped.

Despite having planned to leave the mining industry by the time of the strike, Noman felt he had to join the fight to save people's jobs. Arrested several times, he often had difficulty convincing the police that his surname wasn't a fabrication.

The North-East pits were miles out under the North Sea and it was quite something to see fossilised ferns down there in the tunnels and fossilised trees known as 'glassy backs'. When I was eighteen a group of us were doing advanced heading, meaning we were constantly digging to move forward. A tunnel collapsed and I really thought we'd had it. We were under there for twelve hours and I started to cry but an old miner told me to shut up and eat my sandwiches. He'd seen it all before.

I hated being a miner. The conditions were inhuman, and one year, three days before Christmas, I saw my mate get killed when an underground tram he was on got derailed. He had three kids. Nevertheless when the 1984 strike began I knew it was essential to fight to keep the pits open. I became very active in the strike and was arrested several times. There was a saying, 'Fight for coal or sign the dole.' I picketed all over the country and once held a meeting on the top deck of a bus in London to try to get the bus workers to take industrial action. On another occasion I used Gandhi's tactic of passive resistance and some of us sat in a London road, holding up the traffic. The police threatened but I told them, 'Just f–ing run us over then!' In the end they dragged us out of the way.

After the strike I'd had enough of the mines. Like many others, I'd met new people and seen a different way of life. I wanted to get away from my old life and went to London where, amongst other things, I worked as a stagehand at the Southbank. It was here that, for the first time, I got the chance to listen to classical music, and I particularly remember listening to Beethoven behind the scenes. It was wonderful. I took a degree in Literacy Studies and Linguistics and taught English and drama at secondary school level. There were other jobs, including VSO (voluntary service overseas) where I met my wonderful wife, Anne, a British Paralympic athlete who was awarded the MBE in June 2014. We live in Essex with our son who tries to listen patiently to my stories about the strike. I'm proud of what I did and I hope he is too. I've no regrets and I'd do it again if I had to. Definitely.

1. The Durham banner. This was used in London to mark the funeral of Tony Benn, MP, whose image is portrayed.

2. The Wheldale banner (*courtesy of Northern College*).

3. The Markham Main banner.

4. Ferrymore Ridings banner (*courtesy of Northern College*).

5. Hickleton Branch banner
(*courtesy of Northern College*).

6. Stillingfleet Branch banner
(*courtesy of the NUM*).

GO THOU AND DO LIKEWISE

7. One of the earliest banners. These tended to depict religious themes (*courtesy of the NUM*).

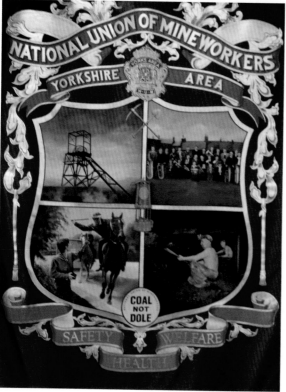

NATIONAL UNION OF MINEWORKERS

YORKSHIRE AREA

COAL NOT DOLE

SAFETY WELFARE HEALTH

8. The NUM's latest banner featuring the now-iconic image by John Harris of Lesley Boulton (*courtesy of the NUM*).

9. Barnsley Miners' Wives Action Group banner (*reproduced with permission of Barnsley Archives & Local Studies*).

10. Badges from the collection of striking Yorkshire miner, Richard Ormrod.

11. Badge to commemorate the deaths of Davy Jones and Joe Green.

12. Silverhill Women's Support Group badge.

13. Cortonwood Women's Action Group badge.

14. Members of the infamous 'snatch squad' in their yellow, high-visibility jackets patrol a Derbyshire street searching for picket-line ringleaders (*courtesy of Bruce Wilson*).

15. Checks, otherwise known as 'tallies', were part of a system used to indicate who was still underground. Each miner was allotted two, one of which would be held by his manager and, until the checks were together again, it was assumed that the miner was still underground.

16. Betty Cook (right) and Anne Scargill of Women Against Pit Closures standing in front of their new banner.

17. Miners emerge at sunrise at the end of their shift, Markham Main Colliery, Armthorpe (*courtesy of Leslie Phillips*).

11

GOING BACK

Charlie Cibor points to a newspaper photograph of himself and his colleagues as they walk back into work at the Markham Main pit in the village of Armthorpe. It was March 1985 and the miners of Markham Main were the last ones in Yorkshire to return to work.

'We were asked to smile for the photo', he explains, 'which we did. Some of us cheered and waved. The minute we turned round the corner, though, out of sight of the photographer, some of the lads started getting tearful. I think we all felt very down – I know I did. We felt proud but down.'

The striking miners were deeply affected by their return to work and this is the topic most likely to affect them even now, thirty years later. Once back at work the strike, for some, was a subject best left alone whilst for the Nottinghamshire and Leicestershire striking miners it was particularly

The miners of Markham Main return to work. Note the brass band in the background (*courtesy of Leslie Phillips*).

A member of the local clergy often attended marches (*courtesy of Leslie Phillips*).

NUM newspaper. The miner waves the figure of a snowman in reference to a trick the pickets had played on police (*courtesy of the NUM*).

important to keep on talking in order to stave off the feelings of isolation brought about by being in a minority group. In some other areas, though, not only were memories just too raw but there was also a strong sense of defeat. The men's feelings were a combination of pride that they had remained strong coupled with a bitterness that they had sacrificed a year's worth of wages for what seemed like nothing. They knew their collieries would be closed soon and that they had lost the fight. For most the future looked grim. Many were suffering from flashbacks, nightmares and depression. Possibly some were suffering from the (then) newly recognised illness, post-traumatic stress disorder.

Miners who had been on strike found, to their dismay, that there was now an increased list of offences for which they could be sacked or fined. Many of these offences were concerned with their attitudes towards those who had worked during the strike.

'You were barely allowed to look at the scabs', continues Charlie, 'and sometimes they would make things up just to get you in trouble. It got ridiculous. It got to the point where you couldn't say anything to them even if it was off pit property. You just weren't allowed to use the word "scab" whatsoever. You could get arrested for saying it wherever you were – not only at work but also in a pub, in a shop, anywhere.'

Some ex-striking miners, however, came up with a simple and novel way to ensure they never accidentally used the 's' word: they used men's names instead. Malcolm Hall of Ollerton (and previously a Durham miner) explains, 'We just called them "Erics" – the police couldn't do anything. We'd say, "There goes another Eric" or "Look out, there's an Eric coming!" We had some fun with it, I can tell you.'

Hundreds had been sacked while those returning to work found that new laws or the re-interpretation of old ones made life difficult. Some found they had to pay various one-off fines, while others discovered that their wages, in effect, had been cut. This made life especially hard for those families whose mortgage payments, along with other debts, had been put on hold during the strike but who now were expected to pay arrears as well as current payments. Many were still living below the breadline for a long time after the end of the strike.

'We were lucky', says Jenny Metcalfe, 'because we had some savings to fall back on. Others got into a terrible mess. Even those of us who did, at least, have some savings, found that the money was pretty soon completely wiped out.'

For the minority of miners who had gone on strike in Nottinghamshire and for the 'Dirty Thirty' of Leicestershire, going back to work brought more than financial problems. It was time for the working miners to take revenge on those who had taken industrial action and who were seen as trouble causers who had brought shame on their non-striking colleagues. Physical attacks were common along with cruel tricks played on former striking miners, which were designed to humiliate. Many managers seemed to take delight in increasing their misery by placing one alone amongst a

The miners of Elsecar Colliery (Yorkshire) return to work (*courtesy of Rhoda Allen*).

group of scabs in order to isolate him. Pat Crowe of Bevercotes Colliery in Nottinghamshire remembers a particularly frightening and emotional moment:

> I was in the cage [lift] going down the shaft. The cages held about thirty men. My boss, the overman, was a nice guy and he'd warned me to watch out for the scabs because they were determined to rile me. At the bottom I got out the cage and there were a gang of 'em waiting for me. They stepped towards me and it looked like they meant business. But then a group of lads, who had

been on strike wi' me, stepped forward from the shadows behind me. They didn't say anything. They didn't need to. But it was like, 'If you touch him you take on all of us.' We were still carrying on looking after one another, see, even though the strike was over.

Many Nottinghamshire and Leicestershire miners agree that what they had to suffer going back to work was worse than anything they had suffered during the strike.

Bob Collier explains:

The working miners, the scabs, couldn't wait to get their revenge on us. They were still convinced that their pits wouldn't close, y'see. They looked upon us striking miners as scum, just like the newspapers – or most of them, anyway – were saying. They said we were responsible for nearly losing them their jobs because of our behaviour. They wanted revenge. It was a very bad time. Worse for us when we went back than owt we'd had to put up with when the strike was on.

Many men returned to work with a show of ceremony despite the knowledge that their colliery would soon be closed down. Banners were brought out and the miners were accompanied by their pit band, often

Silverwood miners return to work (*courtesy of Bruce Wilson*).

along with a member of the local clergy. In many cases wives and families joined the march in a show of support. Whatever the government had inflicted or would inflict upon the striking miners and their families, it was felt that nothing could diminish the brotherhood amongst the men and the declaration of unity and solidarity which had come from the community.

Many never went back. Hundreds were sacked, thus losing their pensions, for having been arrested in the strike and were forced to abandon a generations'-old family tradition. Some used redundancy payments to retrain in vastly different and varied fields. There were those who went ahead and followed a path completely unheard of and never before considered in their traditional coal-mining backgrounds – that of going to university and studying for a degree.

'I never knew I was clever' or 'I never knew I had brains!' are two much-repeated statements by ex-miners who gained their degrees and more often than not entered the teaching profession.

Many of those who were on strike are now in their 80s. The reckless young men who fought on the picket lines and charged through roadblocks are in their 50s. How do they feel now? Was it worth it?

'It was worth it and I'd do it all again', comes the most often repeated reply. 'I thank God I never scabbed,' says one emotional Yorkshire ex-miner, 'I truly learned the meaning of solidarity and my family did too. Our community pulled together and I've got something to pass on to my children, to my grandchildren. We were a part of history and I'm proud.' He wipes his eyes.

Geoffrey Peace, ex-striking miner, is now 80. He worked at Blidworth Colliery, Nottinghamshire, for thirty-eight years. A white-haired, tall man, he sits up straight in his chair and grips his walking stick. He tells his story with a sense of pride and determination.

'At the end people were saying we should ha' done this and we should ha' done that. Well I always say ... WE SHOULD HAVE DONE WHAT WE DID AT THE TIME! Let that be an end to it.'

12

CHARLIE CIBOR

In our last year of school we were sent on various day-release courses to try out different jobs. Most of the lads were destined for the pit or for the army. I was looking forward to becoming a miner and felt proud I'd be carrying on the family tradition. I'd always been genuinely interested in whatever my dad had to say about the pit and his work underground and I had no doubt that this is what I wanted to do. I walked home from my very last day at school relishing the fact that I now had the long school summer holiday ahead of me. It was going to be a great six weeks. I got in, threw my bag down and found my dad was waiting for me with a man I'd never met.

Charlie Cibor, from Yorkshire, followed family tradition by becoming a coal miner. Very active as a picket, he was arrested several times.

'This is your new boss', said my dad. 'You start work Monday.'

Like all the other new recruits I had to take a test. I got a high score and was asked what I wanted to do. Some chose to become electricians but I was determined to work underground. I was put to work on the pit top first where the bosses could suss me out. It was a difficult and dangerous job working underground and not everybody was suited to it. If a problem arose with training then the manager would talk to the lad's father, who was also at the pit, about it first. It's hard to believe now but that's how close this society was. The pit was not only part of your community, it was almost part of your family.

I was put with a few others when I started at the pit and we were all going to be trained together. Well, we looked at one another and decided to dislike each other straight away. We started giving nasty looks to each other and then saying stuff. After a while our manager came over looking annoyed.

'Right you lot!' he bawled, 'I'm sick of listening to you idiots! Come wi' me NOW!'

We all went quiet and followed him. We were wondering what the hell he was going to do. Were we about to lose our jobs?

He took us down the shaft and we ended up in one of the deepest, darkest places you can imagine. 'Now ... all of you, turn your lights off!' he shouted.

We did as he said ... and there was nothing. Pitch black, not a glimmer of light. No sound. It was that quiet you felt as if you could hear the silence. The manager didn't say a word. We waited and we waited. It was like the silence began to make a ringing noise in your ears.

Then he spoke, well ... it was more like a loud whisper, 'Always bear this in mind, you lot. There will come a time when you'll be down here and summat will go wrong. Maybe summat will collapse and you'll be trapped. All you will have is one another.' That was all he said but it really had an effect on us. From that day on we were mates.

During that first year it was instilled into us the dangers we'd be facing. 'There's no way we are going to be carrying you out in a black bag', the boss would say. We were sent to the stockyard where we had to familiarise ourselves with all the equipment we'd be using underground. Later we were sent to work in the bagshed, unloading, loading and stacking sacks. It was filthy, smelly work but it was a good way to build up our muscles to get us ready for the physically demanding work underground. Remember, we were still only 15. Once a week we'd go to a training centre where we were taught about the hazards above and below ground. We were taught so many things: health and safety, fossil fuels, gas explosions, the Davy lamp, first aid. That last would come in useful on the picket line.

We were taken down the pit at intervals just to look at it. Each time we'd be allowed to venture a bit further. It was exciting but forbidding. We were well aware of the possible dangers as, being from mining families, most of us had witnessed pit accident injuries. Every time there was an accident the whole community would pull together, and from a young age you knew that the pit could be a monster which might devour you.

Because the colliery was central to its community it's not surprising that miners' social lives were affected as well. You and your friends would be involved in, for example, sports teams, quiz teams, racing pigeon clubs, brass bands. There were competitions between neighbouring pits and often the whole community would turn out to support their colliery's rugby or football team. All this shows that when we were fighting to keep our pits open, we weren't only fighting for our jobs – we were fighting to keep our community alive.

All this time I was, without realising it, becoming politicised. I went along to NUM meetings with my dad but would always just prefer to sit at the back and listen, taking it all in. He was very political and I suppose I was very much influenced by him. My friends were never very interested in going to meetings or talking politics but I was drawn to it.

When I was 16, in 1972, there was a rumour going round that a big strike was to happen at national level. The miners at our colliery prepared themselves and were ready for action. It was then that I had my first experience on the picket line, and again in 1974. We picketed the power stations to stop coal deliveries, my dad looking after me.

Things were quite ordered on the picket line. We'd be there night and day, camping out in tents. Workers from other nearby companies would come by and donate provisions such as tea and cigarettes. It was here that I first encountered violence between pickets and police. The shape of things to come. We were picketing one night when a police helicopter arrived. Out jumped the police … and made arrests. Nobody ran away. After that I wanted to be more active and urged the others to become more involved. The older men stopped us, saying we were becoming too rowdy and out of control. Through my dad I had come into contact with some senior trades unionists. They were quiet, well-mannered and somehow you knew they had a strength inside them. They taught us that, to get results, we had to be well organised, disciplined and respectable. We young pickets believed in them and followed their example well – until 1984 when we realised, after Orgreave, that there were no rules anymore.

We were all glad to come out on strike in 1984. The older, more experienced miners were telling us that Thatcher was coming for us. By closing Cortonwood the government had thrown down the gauntlet and we had to pick it up. We'd been challenged and we knew we had to rise to that challenge. At first there would be a lot of pushing and shoving between pickets and police lines and there was even some good-humoured banter. Things changed quickly though and the violence increased. The death of Davy Jones changed everything, and then came Orgreave.

The Yorkshire flying pickets went everywhere but our biggest challenge was getting into Nottinghamshire. We used crazy disguises, anything we could think of, to get through the police checks. Once we joined a funeral procession to get over the border and another time we pretended we were escorting a patient to Rampton high-security psychiatric hospital. My mate had somehow managed to get hold of a couple of straightjackets and we used those. It was hilarious at times and we had difficulties keeping a straight face as we were waved through by police.

A lot of pickets would ask the NUM headquarters for daily instructions about where to go. We never did though; instead we relied on intelligence gathering carried out by our lads who were travelling up and down the country. If we heard a particular pit needed help we'd just go. We'd get to Orgreave as often as we could because we knew it was a strategic place. Sometimes we'd picket for a day somewhere and then head to Orgreave straight afterwards. The days were long and it was hard work. Many of us would get home to find our wives and kids in tears because they'd been watching the violence on the TV news.

Picketing was sometimes a nine to five job but more often than not it involved starting in the early hours of the morning to match the shifts that the scabs were working or to try to stop deliveries of coal and coke by the lorries. We started arriving at 4 a.m. but then found other pickets would arrive a bit earlier next day and beat us to it. In the end we all started jokily racing to see who could arrive at a site first. We used to carry out what we called 'night manoeuvres' which involved creating as much havoc as possible to slow the police down next day. Amongst other things we'd slash vehicles' tyres, create roadblocks and spread oil and grease over railings and other surfaces. On one occasion I dug a hole near the colliery gates, climbed in and got my binoculars ready to spy on whoever was going in to work. I wanted to compile a list of scabs' names. After a while the manager stormed over and demanded to know what the hell I was doing. I told him and he replied, 'You silly bugger! Here's the list of names you want ... now bloody well clear off!' – and he gave me the names of the scabs. I rushed back, victorious, to show the list to my mates but it quickly fell to bits because everyone was trying to snatch it. Once we'd learned who the scabs were we devised plans to target them. As far as we were concerned, every man who was working was responsible for others losing their jobs. Every miner that scabbed was pushing a knife in the back of those who were fighting to protect our pits.

I came up with the idea of making paint 'bombs' to lob at scabs' houses so that they'd be marked out for the rest of the community to see. I decided bright pink and yellow would be the best colours for the job. A group of us put bricks and poured paint into plastic carrier bags, the idea being to chuck them at scabs' houses where they'd burst open and leave psychedelic splatters over the doors, windows and walls. We crept towards the houses because, although we were under cover of darkness, we still had to avoid police who were everywhere. At about 2 a.m. a police car spotted us. We held our breath as it slowed down but then, thankfully, it pulled away. We were doing well until my brother realised that his bag had a leak and, as he threw it, it burst open all over him. We were laughing so much as we retraced our steps – which wasn't difficult because we were able to follow the leaking paint trail. We made a lot of noise and lights came on in all the surrounding houses. Next day we made the local TV news.

One night I'd managed to get hold of some fireworks. Much of the day's picketing was over and the police were sitting in their cars drinking coffee. I crept round to the side of the car park and let off this enormous repeating banger. The police dived for cover and so did the few lads left on the picket line. I stood, arms folded, laughing at the scene until the police spotted me and, realising what I'd done, gave chase. They were furious and were determined to get me. I thought they would kill me but I somehow got away. My mates and me were always carrying out stunts like this and the older miners nicknamed us the 'Red Squad'. They thought we were crazy – and maybe we were.

There was one day when we found there was a massive wall of police in riot gear facing us. They'd formed a crescent shape so that they were at the sides of us as well, like a pincer movement. Anyway, that film *Zulu* had been on telly. The cops started banging their shields, softly at first but getting louder and louder until the noise was deafening. At the same time they were shouting, 'Zuuuluu!' There was summat threatening about it but at the same time I remember thinking this was one of the most incredible things I'd ever seen. It was just amazing. Me and my mates stood there like we were transfixed, our mouths open. Not for long, though. The police charged and we had to run like hell ... The police were eventually banned from banging their shields by the powers that be because it wasn't professional! Makes you laugh, that.

When it came to Orgreave there was none of the fun and games. In the end it all came down to having guts. It was nicknamed the 'Battle of Orgreave' but this wasn't just a nickname, it was the real thing. It was a battle. None of us could believe what we were seeing when the horses charged out of police lines. We were totally unprepared. The news reporters there were terrified and were running away. A group of us managed to run into the grounds of a small building and closed the gates but the horses just burst straight through. We fought hand-to-hand, one-on-one battles with officers. It was almost impossible to get to them though because they were dressed in full riot gear with helmets, visors, the lot. We'd try to run because we knew they had weapons whereas we had nothing and we were very vulnerable in our T-shirts and jeans. If they caught up with you they'd truncheon you on the back of the legs to bring you down ... It was intensely painful and I saw lads screaming. All our first-aid training at the pit came in useful as we tried to help others who had come down or collapsed. We tried to help the injured ourselves because we knew that, if they were taken to hospital, they'd be arrested. Orgreave finished a lot of men off for a while. They'd been badly physically injured and mentally scarred. We now realised we were involved in a civil war. Although some of us needed time to recover from Orgreave, we came back. We would always, always come back.

13

GHOSTS

Walking along the track leading to what was Cortonwood Colliery is a cheerless experience even on a bright spring day when daffodils are blooming. A soulless warehouse now occupies the site of the colliery, and the trackway, once echoing with the sound of miners' tramping boots, is covered in litter. The place has become something of an illegal dumping ground where plastic bottles and parts of broken toys are blown about in the breeze while soiled disposable nappies and some old, stained cushions are left to rot. Shreds of clothing are caught up in bushes along the path, fluttering like the remnants of flags from some long-ago battle.

A 1920s leaflet explaining the history of coal mining.

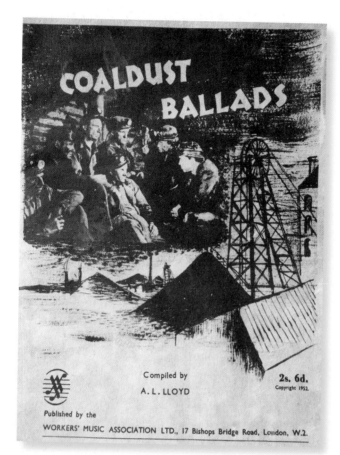

Music has always played an important rôle in mining communities. This sheet music would have been used by the colliery's brass band and choir.

At the other end of the trackway several large, rectangular concrete blocks have been grouped together to form a barrier against, presumably, travellers wishing to set up camp. It does not require too much imagination to feel that, somehow, the blocks are reminiscent of gravestones. Beyond the blocks is the road where in the spring of 1984 lines of police awaited the arrival of hundreds of pickets. The council has erected a low wall running along part of the length of this road on which are carvings illustrating the history of the area through the centuries. The last design features, in small lettering, the simple words, 'The Alamo'. No explanation is provided. Perhaps some feel it is better forgotten.

A few miles away in Armthorpe, Markham Main Colliery, the scene of so many pitched battles, is now submerged under a modern housing estate. A small concrete post giving brief details of the colliery is the only

Small sign on the wall near Cortonwood.

The rubbish-strewn entrance to Cortonwood.

Demolition of Markham Main Colliery (*courtesy of Leslie Phillips*).

acknowledgement that here once stood what was the life-blood of the community. The site of the 'Battle of Orgreave' has also been built upon and the surrounding landscape is almost unrecognisable when compared to how it looked in 1984. The slagheaps which once defined the landscape of this part of Yorkshire have been grassed over and, perhaps symbolically, resemble large Neolithic burial grounds.

'You've heard of Stone-Age burial mounds?', one old miner asks, 'Well these are Coal-Age burial mounds.'

Cortonwood memorial.

Markham Main Memorial Garden.

Memorial outside the NUM headquarters, Barnsley.

Aerial view of Markham Main Colliery, Armthorpe (*c.*1994). The shadow of the winding gear falls across the old steam house. The reservoir, upper right, was used for the cooling towers. During the 1950s local children often used it as a swimming pool until, tragically, one young girl drowned. The pit housing estate can be seen at the top of the picture (*courtesy of Leslie Phillips*).

Former pit-villages are determined that their way of life should be remembered. Welfare clubs still exist and provide entertainment and events which still bind the community together. Archive and resource centres have been set up and are run by ex-striking miners and their families. Statues, sculptures and memorial gardens have been created and every year there are celebratory marches and galas in former mining areas,

Pit showers (*courtesy of Leslie Phillips*).

The lamp room, Silverwood Colliery (*courtesy of Bruce Wilson*).

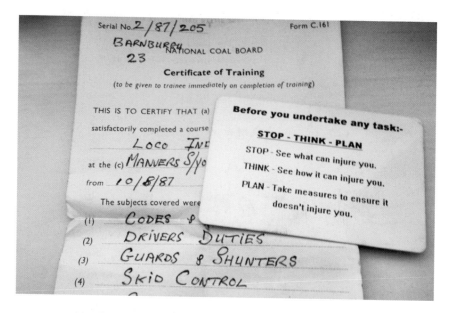

Training certificate (*courtesy of Roger Hackleton*).

Old-style phone which would have been used underground (*courtesy of Aylesham Resource Centre*).

Memorial plates are still collected by the mining community and some command high prices such as the Cortonwood plate.

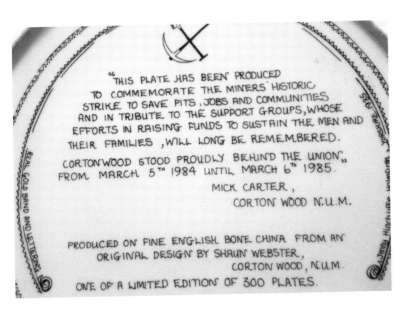

often attracting many thousands of people. Coal mining was once, quite literally, the bedrock of British industry. Although the miners' strike of 1984 failed to save that industry, it is fast becoming entrenched in the country's history as one of the most important socio-industrial episodes, rivalling Peterloo, the Tolpuddle Martyrs and the 1926 General Strike. Time will tell.

14

THE CHILDREN ... AND THE NEXT GENERATION

No One Knows But Her

She's alone her mind ticking over
The problems she's got to face
No money, no food, no coal,
Maybe soon no home

She's alone with wandering thoughts
She cries a little and sighs a little
I wish I could get inside her mind
To ease the pain and make it better

She's alone shaking her head
I know that she's got it solved
But what keeps her going
She's a stayer she's strong
She's my mother

Vicky Curry, aged 10 (1984)

Those who have childhood memories of the strike are now in their 30s or 40s and many have children of their own. They say that it is only now, since they have become parents themselves, that they realise how hard it was for their mothers and fathers. It seems that the vast majority of parents did their utmost to shield their children from the worst aspects of the strike but it was often hard to protect them from the reality of the situation when food was in short supply and there was no heating. Aggie Curry is still moved to tears whenever she recounts how she would be forced to make the choice between giving supper or breakfast to her children:

> They often either had to go to bed hungry or set off for school in the morning without breakfast. No mother should have to make these choices and people who weren't going through it couldn't believe that this was happening in modern-day Britain. Thatcher thought that if she could get to the mothers by hurting the children, then the strike would quickly come to an end. But there were many women like me who would not give in. We were rock solid. In the long term we were doing this for our kids because we knew that if the pits closed, there would be no jobs for them and their lives would be wrecked. We weren't just being stubborn by supporting the strike, we were doing it because we loved our kids.

Children went hungry and children were cold. They were denied the treats which are often seen as a routine part of childhood such as holidays and birthday presents. Yet they rarely complained because, it seems, they realised that they were part of something bigger and something unprecedented. Their friends, their peer groups, were all experiencing the same deprivations and hardships and this made the situation easier to bear. The ones who did have enough materially were suffering the isolation of being ostracised by the others because their fathers were labelled as scabs. As the strike wore on and gained international support, the children were increasingly receiving gifts of toys, clothes and food. Many were taken for trips abroad by their parents

as guests of foreign trades unions and mining communities. As for Christmas, the most common memory is that 'It was the best Christmas I ever had!' The adults pulled together in a massive effort and it was exciting for the children to be eating their Christmas dinner en masse with all the other local families in the community

Kay Foster with her sister, Kerry, in 1984 (*courtesy of Kay Foster*).

120

hall or welfare club. Shows, pantomimes and carol services were organised, with Father Christmas making several appearances to hand out presents which had arrived from around the world.

Throughout all this, however, many adults knew that the end they had been fearing was inevitable. An increasing number were returning to work and there was no show of the much-needed support from other unions, which might, just might, have saved the day. It was a grim time and, as often happens, children were quick to pick up on the fact that their parents were worried and afraid. Mothers, and often fathers, could be heard crying during the night and there would be arguments as the stress became too much.

This moving extract from a school essay written by Aggie Curry's daughter, Vicky, then aged 10, illustrates how children were aware of their parents' suffering and difficulties:

> Well I don't really understand a lot about the strike but I do know that my dad and mum are standing up for what they believe in. It is so me and my brother Peter can work when we leave school. My mum goes on the picket line. One copper smacked her and she lost her tooth. I some times hear my mum crying at night because she can't get us a lot for Christmas. My dad says don't worry love the kids will be alright. I don't want my mum to meet maggie or Megeror she says she will ring their bloodie necks *[sic]*. My dad says that when we start work we must never cross a picket line as our gran and grandad went without in 1926 so we could have what we have today.

Because the strike had taken over people's lives it was often considered better to let the children join in with many of the activities centred on fundraising and marching. As might be expected, the children loved it. Sharon Johnson, the daughter of a South Kirkby striking miner, remembers accompanying her father on a march to Frickley football ground to hear Arthur Scargill speak. Her father was part of a group of pickets who called themselves 'Logan's Run' and were written about in a London local newspaper after they had been fundraising there. Kay Foster would be taken annually to join the David Jones memorial marches in South Kirby or South Elmsall and has clear memories of her father chatting to Arthur Scargill in 1984 about Scargill's arrest at Orgreave.

Many children were allowed to join in with coal-picking, which they tended to view as a fun family activity rather than a chore. Sharon Johnson remembers she was allowed to join in when her family and neighbours hired a van and '... went coal-picking for twelve hours solid'.

Striking miners' children, now adults, all retain a strong sense of pride in their fathers and, indeed, their mothers. For many, like Sharon Johnson, the pride is mixed with sadness and regret that their parents' lives were forever blighted by the closure of their collieries:

> Dad got a job as a factory cleaner when his pit closed. He felt a bit useless because hard work was all he ever knew. To be honest, he lost his spark and sort of gave up. It was physical as well because he seemed to shrink in size, like he was defeated.

Because whole communities were involved in the strike, the after-effects have inevitably trickled down through to younger generations who were not even born at the time. Kylie Wroe, from Barnsley, remembers there always being the sense of a still-open wound as she grew up in the 1990s:

> My dad wasn't even a miner but I grew up hearing his stories about how he'd go coal-picking and how awful it was for him to see friends and neighbours experiencing such poverty. The house I grew up in wasn't far from Cortonwood: I just knew it as 'The Alamo', even though I didn't know what that meant until years later. Looking back, I remember a feeling of rawness, of unfinished business and sadness in the community.

Recently an even younger generation has taken up the torch, as it were, and children are learning in school about their grandparents' experiences during the strike. Hopefully one day they will pass their knowledge on to their own children.

Adam Metcalfe, grandson of Derbyshire striking miner Ian Metcalfe.

15

'TRAPPED IN TIME' BY BRUCE WILSON

Bruce Wilson, a Yorkshire miner, was a picket and activist during the strike.

A favourite time for me was on the Sunday night-shift when the deputy would take me with him on his walks round the old roadways and mine workings and we would go exploring. As we ventured into these time warps, the deputy would put his initials and the date in chalk on an old girder to show he'd been there. This was 1982 and on these steel girders, supporting the old roadway, you would see the initials of a mine official from, for example, 1932. You felt like if you went round the corner, you'd bump into the man who had left his mark. Some of the old coal faces and roadways dated from before the First World War. They were just as men had left them all those years ago.

There were dudleys (metal drinking bottles), pit props and all sorts lying about as if waiting for the men to come back. You would come to an old coalface, maybe 3ft high with wooden supports. I'd pick up a bit of newspaper from the floor and it might be *News of the World* from 1928. If you took it out of the mine, though, it would just disintegrate.

Once we came to an old pit-pony stables, a real time warp. The roadway entrance was about 5ft high, 8ft wide and had a superbly made wooden door. The stables were so immaculate you could have eaten your dinner off the floor. Hanging on the white-washed walls was the pony tack, the harnesses and so on. The ponies' names were painted perfectly on a square wooden board, fixed to the rear of their stables. It was as if everything was waiting for their return at the end of a shift. The elements couldn't reach down here and everything was 'trapped in time'.

16

JOHN HARRIS, PHOTOGRAPHER

John Harris produced some of the strike's most startling and controversial photographs, including the now-iconic image of a mounted police officer in riot gear about to strike a cowering Lesley Boulton with his truncheon. (See plate 8)

I was pleased when, at 26, my agency assigned me to cover the miners' strike as I knew, perhaps almost instinctively, that the strike would have far-reaching consequences.

I'd covered the Toxteth riots three years earlier, so I felt that at least I was more experienced than some in dealing with scenes of violent confrontation. Months into the miners' strike, however, the stress of my work began to take its toll and I was aware that I was pushing myself to, and in some cases beyond, my limits. I was constantly placing myself in dangerous situations in order to get that one last shot before running for cover. This was a war zone, though, and this is what war zone photographers do.

If the strike was a turning point in our history, Orgreave was a turning point in the strike. Yes, Orgreave was frightening but, in some ways, what I found more threatening, more chilling, were the night-time episodes when I'd somehow become isolated in the darkness, knowing the enemy was somewhere close. The police hated me because I'd been taking shots of them beating up pickets and chasing women and kids. They had me down as a marked man. Many of the photographers would finish at the end of the day and get their pictures sent off (no Internet in those days!) to meet a deadline. I was never really that concerned about deadlines: I was more concerned about documenting the truth. I'd often stay much later and then find I was alone and lost. I remember an episode where I was hopelessly wandering around the maze of a modern housing estate, trying to find a way out. There was no one around. It was desolate and very dark because the street lights were off. A police van slowly cruised up behind me and crawled along beside me at walking pace for quite some time. I couldn't see their faces and it was intimidating, sinister. I was genuinely afraid of what might happen and, even today, I try not to think of it because the feeling comes flooding back.

Darkness, of course, was a photographer's nightmare. I was at Cortonwood at night or in the early hours of the morning when the only light came from police vans' headlights. The vans were repeatedly being driven straight into the crowds of pickets and bystanders and I wanted to get this on film. The trouble was that, as soon as the flash went off, the police would instantly know you were a photographer and would come for you. I got some very ethereal-looking shots of figures half in, half out of shadow as the vans' headlights picked them out.

It wasn't just the police who hated me. The pickets, who were being given a very hard time by the media, pretty much loathed me as well. It did get better later when some of them got to know me and realised I wasn't part of Murdoch's lot. There were times that summer, though, when I found myself physically caught between the police, who would clobber me if they could and the pickets, who probably felt like punching me (they never did).

Yes, Orgreave was a turning point. I'd been going most weeks and always kept to the designated press area. One day a picket, who was being dragged off by police, spotted me and shouted, 'Ayup mate! Why don't you go up there and see what's really happening! This is nowt compared to what's goin' on over there!' So I thought, 'Sod it, why don't I!' and, defying the police, set off. I hid my camera (which was wrecked by the end of the strike) and went over to where the real action was going on. Orgreave was, indeed, a battle, in the fullest sense of the word. There were repeated charges, withdrawals and regroupings throughout the day. The initial charge on horseback had happened when rows of riot police had parted to let the horses come through. Later on the police would, every now and then, take great delight in pretending to part so that the pickets would start to run. The police thought this was a great joke. Gradually, throughout the day, many of the pickets were herded to the end of the field. It was a kind of mass kettling procedure. At one point, during a lull, I went off to get a cup of tea in the village. When I returned it was utter mayhem and I'd missed a great chunk of it. Damn. Later, when I was running from a police charge through the village, an old lady ushered me through her front door and hid me in her cupboard under the stairs. I'd learned that, if you adopted an air of insouciance, casually walking around, camera out of the way, apparently relaxed, you could often keep below the police radar. Sometimes, however, you knew you just had to get the hell out of there. Much of the time, in these sort of situations, a photographer's fear is suppressed and overridden by the responsibility of being a news-gatherer. You become so immersed in what you're doing that, it's only when you feel sweat trickling down your neck and back and wonder whether it is blood, you realise you're scared. I wasn't just able to get on with my work; I was also desperately trying to avoid being clobbered by the police or knocked down and trampled on by a horse (which did happen to me).

I saw Lesley Boulton and a photographer trying to help the injured guy on the ground. The cop on horseback was coming towards them, baton raised, so I click-clicked. That was it. No time for preparation as I was well aware that, just behind my right shoulder, there was another mounted officer ready to deal with me. Many people don't realise that, at the extreme left edge of the photo, there's a hand stretching out to grab Lesley to pull her down, just in time, out of harm's way. The *Observer* newspaper's publishing that photo resulted in police facing a disciplinary enquiry.

Months of tension, high emotion, physical injury and lack of sleep led to near burnout for me towards the end of the strike. The effects on me took a long time to subside and have never been fully erased. Every picket would, no doubt, say the same.

(Photography by John Harris can be found on his agency's website: reportdigital.co.uk.)

CONCLUSION

The 1984/5 miners' strike was not only about saving jobs; it was also an attempt to protect communities and preserve a way of life. The strike has become a symbol of the working-class movement because, once the National Union of Mineworkers had been stripped of its power, other unions became weaker as they had depended on the NUM to back them. Without strong unions, working-class people were, to a large extent, left without a voice. This, along with Margaret Thatcher's economic policies, meant that traditional working-class societies began a long process of disintegration that many would argue is still continuing today.

With the NUM and, therefore, other unions no longer a threat, Margaret Thatcher set about steering the UK to follow the doctrine of neoliberalism, where privatisation became the watchword of her government. This system offered huge financial rewards to those individuals who were strong enough to enter the race where winner takes all. Two of the remaining deep pit mines that survived the mass closure of the collieries, Kellingley in Yorkshire and Thoresby in Nottinghamshire, were privatised and are owned by UK Coal, while the third, Hatfield in South Yorkshire, is run by an employee benefit trust. Kellingley and Thoresby are under threat of closure and Britain now imports coal from abroad.

The negative environmental impact of burning fossil fuels has become an increasing area of concern, though there are those who believe that coal can be 'cleaned' by using processes to eliminate damaging chemicals. Meanwhile the coal seams have been abandoned along with heavy-duty mining equipment and vehicles left underground because salvage costs are too high. The closure of the collieries was on such a vast scale and was so swift that social-historians and economists are still assessing the ramifications. The striking miners themselves sometimes point out that, 'If you weren't part of it you won't understand'. Hopefully the songs, poems and stories written about the mining industry, including the strike, will remain as valuable witness to a bygone era.

BIBLIOGRAPHY

Arkell, Peter & Ray Rising, *Unfinished Business: The Miners' Strike for Jobs 1984–5* (Lupus Books, 2009)

Bell, David, *The Dirty Thirty: Heroes of the Miners' Strike* (Five Leaves, 2009)

Bell, David, *Memories of the Nottinghamshire Coalfields* (Countryside Books, 2008)

Holden, Triona, *Queen Coal: Women of the Miners' Strike* (Sutton Pubishing Limited, 2005)

Metcalf, Mark, Martin Jenkinson & Mark Harvey, *Images of the Past: The Miners' Strike* (Pen & Sword History, 2014)

Milne, Seumas, *The Enemy Within: The Secret War Against the Miners, 30th Anniversary Edition* (Verso Books, 2014)

National Union of Mineworkers, *A Century of Struggle: Britain's Miners in Pictures 1889–1989* (NUM, 1989)

National Union of Mineworkers, *The Miner: Journal of the National Union of Mineworkers* (NUM 1984-5)

Paterson, Harry, *Look Back in Anger: The Miners' Strike in Nottinghamshire 30 Years On* (Five Leaves, 2014)

Simons, Mike, *Striking Back: Photographs of the Great Miners' Strike 1984–1985* (Bookmarks Publications Ltd, 2004)